Cup Overflowing

Wine's Place in Faith, Feasting, and Fellowship

Gisela H. Kreglinger

ZONDERVAN REFLECTIVE

ZONDERVAN REFLECTIVE

Cup Overflowing
Copyright © 2024 by Gisela H. Kreglinger

Published in Grand Rapids, Michigan, by Zondervan. Zondervan is a registered trademark of The Zondervan Corporation, L.L.C., a wholly owned subsidiary of HarperCollins Christian Publishing, Inc.

Requests for information should be addressed to customercare@harpercollins.com.

Zondervan titles may be purchased in bulk for educational, business, fundraising, or sales promotional use. For information, please email SpecialMarkets@Zondervan.com.

ISBN 978-0-310-13448-0 (softcover)
ISBN 978-0-310-13450-3 (audio)
ISBN 978-0-310-13449-7 (ebook)

Cover design and photography: Micah Kandros
Interior design: Sara Colley

Printed in the United States of America

24 25 26 27 28 LBC 5 4 3 2 1

Once more Gisela Kreglinger's gifts of clarity, enthusiasm, and scholarship come to the fore in this new book, an exploration and celebration of wine's central place in faith and Scripture. She writes as much for the sceptic as for the enthusiast, showing a real understanding of how and why temperance movements have arisen, and making the case for moderation as itself part of the pleasure and celebration of wine. There is rich history here, together with wisdom and philosophy but also a great deal of practical help and advice for creating and sustaining a healthy drinking culture.

—MALCOLM GUITE, POET, PRIEST, AND SCHOLAR

Gisela Kreglinger is religious and I'm not, which did not at all stop me from enjoying her delicious new release much more than most contemporary wine books. Too often we are expected to appreciate someone's personal "tasting notes"—how boring! Gisela's book is not a guide, more like a path. With a welcome simplicity and joyous spirituality, she delivers profound reflections on wine's place in our culture. Her take on the biblical view of wine surprised and delighted me, deepening my appreciation of wine's place in my own life.

—KERMIT LYNCH, WINE MERCHANT; AUTHOR,
ADVENTURES ON THE WINE ROUTE

While wine imparts the Spirit's blessing and joy, we find ways to foolishly misuse the gift and inflict harm. Thankfully, we have Gisela Kreglinger, a wise and generous theologian, to guide us into wholeness and abundance.

—WINN COLLIER, DIRECTOR, EUGENE PETERSON CENTER
FOR CHRISTIAN IMAGINATION; AUTHOR, *A BURNING IN MY
BONES: THE AUTHORIZED BIOGRAPHY OF EUGENE PETERSON*

I was so excited to read *Cup Overflowing* by my friend Gisela Kreglinger, and it did not disappoint! Gisela is one of the smartest people I know, and this book is a fascinating deep dive into the role of wine in Christian spirituality. For Christian professionals, *Cup Overflowing* offers a profound reminder that our work and celebrations can be imbued with divine joy and purpose, transforming ordinary moments into sacred experiences that deepen our connection with God and each other. I highly recommend it!

—JORDAN RAYNOR, AUTHOR, *THE SACREDNESS OF SECULAR WORK* AND *REDEEMING YOUR TIME*

Gisela provides a robust theological, historical, cultural, and biblical picture of all that God has to teach us through wine—and all that is at stake when we fail to steward this gift well. It's so easy to approach consumption with an all-or-nothing attitude, wanting to categorize foods and drinks as wholly good or wholly bad. Gisela resists that compulsion, instead teaching us that to respect God's gift of wine, we must understand its limits (and our own). This book is a gift both to those who already love and appreciate wine and to those who are unsure how alcohol fits into the Christian life. I hope you'll read it while savoring a glass!

—KENDALL VANDERSLICE, AUTHOR, *BAKE AND PRAY*; THEOLOGIAN; BAKER

Combining engaging personal and historical stories, Kreglinger makes space at our theological table for wine and its profound significance for our lives and spiritual growth. This book reminds us of what it means to feast with the Bridegroom, drink at the Lord's Supper, and rejoice in God's Kingdom, forever savoring the wonder and hope of God. I encourage everyone to drink the insights of this book deeply!

—BETH STOVELL, PROFESSOR OF OLD TESTAMENT AND CHAIR OF GENERAL THEOLOGICAL STUDIES AT AMBROSE UNIVERSITY, NATIONAL THEOLOGICAL CONSULTANT FOR VINEYARD CANADA

Cup Overflowing

My cup overfloweth:

For my husband, Roy,
for it was the convivial Spirit who
brought us together at the table,
with friends, food, and some rather well-crafted wine.

Contents

Acknowledgments

This book has emerged out of my life growing up on a family-run winery in Bavaria, Germany, and my vocation devoted to exploring and teaching a Christian spirituality that is rooted in the Bible and God's good creation. My teachers, Gordon Fee, Richard Bauckham, and Eugene Peterson, insisted that Christian spirituality must emerge from the truths and storied patterns of the Bible. I am grateful for this rich community of mentors, teachers, and friends who shaped my life and vocation so profoundly.

In the beginning, this book was envisioned to make material from my previous book, *The Spirituality of Wine*, available to a wider readership. In the process of writing, this book took on its own dynamic and now addresses more specifically the cultural context of North America, where I now live and have made my home once more. The US has its own history and journey with wine and alcohol more widely speaking. It is important to understand it and trust that God can, and desires to, redeem it. I interviewed a range of Christians about their relationship and struggles with wine and alcohol. Some of these conversations were sobering. I am grateful for their honest contributions and hope that these stories will help us think carefully about how to develop a more wholesome relationship with wine.

I am grateful for a rich Christian community that has supported me in this work: my writer's group, Rebecca Poe Hays and Rachel Toombs. Your feedback and insight have made this work more nuanced. Thank you to Poul Guttesen for reading various parts of the manuscript and giving me such helpful feedback. I thank Katya Covrett and David McNutt at Zondervan for their editorial help. To these and so many of my friends, colleagues, and students I am deeply grateful for the conversations and prayers that have enriched my praying, thinking, and writing.

Introduction

This book might come as a surprise to you. Why should you read a book about the spirituality of wine? What role might wine have in the life of the church? As Christians, aren't we committed to truly spiritual things, building up the body of Christ and seeing the kingdom of God coming down to earth? Surely wine doesn't have anything to do with that. Doesn't the apostle Paul even remind us that the kingdom of God is not about eating and drinking but about spiritual things such as righteousness and peace and joy in the Holy Spirit (Rom. 14:17)?

This is not an uncommon response I get when I tell people that I write and speak about the theology and spirituality of wine. I have to remind them that Jesus' first miracle was turning water into wine. He miracled forth such an abundance of really high-end, high-quality wine at a Jewish peasant wedding feast that the sommelier at the party was astounded. Did you know that Jesus drank four cups of wine when he celebrated the Passover meal with his disciples? He was known to hang out with the rough and ready of society, enjoying wine with saints and sinners alike. He surely did not fit into the spiritual vision of his own people and offended the religious status quo seemingly wherever he went.

I always feel a bit jarred when I have these conversations because I did not grow up in a Christian culture where drinking wine was ever an issue. The world of wine and the world of faith have always been profoundly interwoven in my culture and my family in Franconia, Germany. I grew up in a Lutheran family that has run a winery for many generations. We turned Lutheran when the Reformation teaching reached us in the early seventeenth century, and as far as I know those early pioneering Lutherans continued to craft wine just as the nuns and monks had done before them. It is a rich heritage, and I am deeply grateful for it.

You might come from the opposite end of the spectrum, where the worlds of wine and faith have traditionally been strictly, or perhaps not so strictly, separated. Do you feel uncomfortable with the idea that wine is a spiritual gift? Perhaps you feel slightly sinful for indulging in a glass of wine or overly afraid that wine might be the devil's tool of temptation. Whatever your background might be, these beautiful and mysterious worlds of wine and faith never should have been severed from one another. They've belonged together ever since Noah planted his first vineyard close to the mountains of Ararat. Though Noah was also the first person in the Bible to get drunk, his vocation as a vintner set the stage for wine to become the most talked about food in the Bible.

As one who is fully at home in the world of wine and in Christian faith, I felt a responsibility to help bring those two worlds back together and allow joy to take its rightful place in our Christian communities.

The Bible is saturated with talk about wine, and so is the history of the church. Up until the nineteenth century, all Christian traditions used wine in the Lord's Supper. It was only after Thomas Bramwell Welch discovered pasteurization in the nineteenth century that the world learned how to keep grape juice from fermenting into wine. Grape juice in the Lord's Supper is still a recent phenomenon in the grand scale of things.

Growing up, I had never even heard of Christian traditions that did not serve wine in the Lord's Supper or did not drink wine at the dinner table and on festive occasions. It came as a bit of shock to me when, after many years of studying theology, I moved across the ocean to take up a teaching position at a seminary in the American South. Upon arrival, I was informed about their "dry campus." I was a little confused. *Did they not have enough water to irrigate the perfectly manicured lawns?* Oh no, they had plenty of water for that.

I learned that a dry campus is where no one is allowed to bring and consume alcohol. *Good grief,* I thought. *That is quite radical.* I had never heard of such a thing.

In Europe, most institutions of culture and learning, including universities and divinity schools, offer wine receptions after important events. Some of the most interesting conversations and learning experiences happen as people sip a glass of wine together. In my new cultural setting, not even at faculty retreats were we allowed a glass of wine with dinner, and the atmosphere remained rather formal and polite. I missed the ease and convivial atmosphere that wine receptions bring to the often rather sober and stiff environment that seems to haunt academic settings.

The faculty retreat, however, was my introduction to the undercurrents of formal Southern culture. Some of my younger colleagues had done their studies in Scotland, and PhDs weren't the only things they acquired there. Alongside their laborsome studies, they had developed a taste not only for wine but also whiskey and the conviviality and joy they can elicit within us. Very tactfully, a little underground group was organized, and after the official retreat program, colleagues gathered in one of the rooms to savor the forbidden fruit in the form of wine and whiskey. It was all done very discreetly and brought ease to my soul as I struggled with culture shock and worries of how I would ever fit into this foreign culture.

I also learned quickly that the dry campus was not quite as dry as they made us believe. Students, especially the undergrads, didn't always keep to the rules. I guess they enjoyed pushing against boundaries just to see what happened. Apparently, the resident students smuggled in plenty of booze on campus, but it wasn't the good stuff. It was cheap beer, cheap wine, and lots of cheap spirits, all the things my family does not approve of and taught me to stay away from. My family strives so hard to educate our customers about the importance of quality wine. We believe that savoring a beautiful wine slowly can and should enrich our spiritual lives, deepen bonds of friendship, and open our eyes to the wonders around us.

The students had not discovered such delights and settled for gulping down cheap alcohol. It made me sad. I found myself in a

Christian cultural setting that did not make room for developing a healthy and wholesome relationship with wine. I felt there was a void. It was one of my postgraduate students who helped me understand a bit more of why my host country had come to have such an ambivalent posture toward wine and alcohol. As is often the case, there is a whole history to it. I have to admit it was tempting for me to become judgmental and cynical about it and not push harder into understanding the background to it all.

Lucie came to see me in my office. As a class we had explored the ministry of hospitality together and the students had to watch a film called *Babette's Feast*. In this film generous amounts of wine are served as part of a lavish meal bestowed upon an ascetical and pietistic Lutheran community. Subtle references to the exodus, the Jewish Passover meal, and the Lord's Supper are woven into the fabric of the whole narrative. The film is a resounding affirmation of wine and food as spiritual gifts that God can use to bring a Christian community back together and help them overcome bitterness, anger, and resentment. While some loved the film, others were rather disturbed by it. It upset something deep inside of them, something that had been passed on from one generation to another.

Lucie was one of them. She felt torn in how to handle the whole wine and alcohol question. Her parents and her grandparents never touched alcohol and did not approve of drinking alcohol at all. As she explored this subject in one of her papers, she felt she was somehow betraying her family if she decided that wine in the Bible was indeed actual alcoholic wine and that it was okay for her to drink it and share it around the dinner table.

Lucie's grandfather had grown up with an alcoholic father whose addiction to cheap moonshine spirits wreaked havoc in the family. His addiction made him violent and unpredictable. He wasn't able to hold down a job for very long and the family struggled in severe poverty. These early experiences deeply traumatized her grandfather. It's as if the trauma never left him and settled deep into the crevices of his soul. Lucie told me that he still has a hard time expressing his emotions, and without warning, anger can flare up in him and he will lash out against those closest to him.

A devoted follower of Jesus and an ardent student of the Bible, Lucie's grandfather loves retelling her favorite Bible stories, and she loves listening to him. His Baptist faith has anchored him in a reality saturated by love and grace, and yet at times something deep inside still pulls him right back into those dark places. His devotion to God and his family, his hard work and disciplined lifestyle provided the foundation for his own children and grandchildren to flourish. They were able to let go of the traumas of the past that he still holds inside.

When Lucie tried to talk to her grandfather about wine in the Bible, there was no reasoning with him. He became agitated and frustrated with her, insisting that wine in the Bible wasn't wine at all but grape juice. At other times he would sway a bit and say that really in the Bible wine was very diluted and had hardly any alcohol in it. In the end, Lucie gave up and now avoids talking about wine with the family altogether. We had some good conversations as she went on this journey of discovery, and I learned a great deal not only about her family but also about a whole culture that had been traumatized by alcohol abuse.

Listening to story after story like this, I began to realize that North America has had a particular history with alcohol and alcohol abuse. When settlers first arrived on the shores of the Americas, they tried to grow vines and craft wine just as they had done in their home countries. However, the climate on the east coast wasn't suitable for the vines they had brought from Europe, and prolonged and repeated efforts continued to fail. The wine they did have was imported from Europe, and that was of course expensive and only the upper class could afford it.

What they did manage quite easily is to set up distilleries to make strong spirits, and whiskey became the primary drink of the average American in the early nineteenth century. When the Civil War wrought havoc among the American people in the latter part of the century, a whole generation became traumatized, and many must have turned to whiskey to find solace and escape. The widespread abuse of strong spirits after the Civil War led to Prohibition in the early twentieth century, something that Europe has never experienced. Strong spirits were never the primary drink for the average European in France, Germany, or Italy, for example. North America has a unique history with particular and unfortunate constellations. Had they been able to make wine on the east coast of the United States before the war, the story might have been very different.

Listening to many more stories of my students and colleagues and learning of this particular history made me more compassionate and understanding. But times have changed. We have to learn to own our stories, embrace the healing that must happen, and move on to a more wholesome way of dealing with life. Trauma can be healed. Removing ourselves from the tensions of life will not allow us to grow and mature. Nor does the Bible promote such an approach to the spiritual life. There are nearly one thousand references to wine and wine-related themes in the Bible. The Bible affirms wine as a gift from God. Wine, like power, success, sex, work, money, food, and so many other good things in life can become places of temptation and pull us into the downward spiral of addiction. Removing ourselves from them doesn't need to be the answer. Life is wrought with great tensions and temptations, and it is in these tensions and temptations that Christ wants to meet us with love and grace, heal us and mature us into sainthood, inch by inch.

Perhaps you come from just such a context and would like to learn about how wine and the Christian life fit together. Or perhaps you come from a context in which this wasn't a pressing question for you. Regardless, there is still much to learn about how we can reclaim wine as a gift from God. What I would like to do in this book is introduce you to wine as a spiritual gift. God gave wine to bless us, to bring us joy and help us draw near to him. Christ lifted the cup of wine to yet greater glories when he offered it to his disciples as his blood, rich in fragrance and salvation. My prayer is that this book will inspire you to experience more fully one of God's earthly gifts and help you to commune more deeply with the creator of all good things.

PART 1

WHAT WOULD JESUS DRINK?

Tracing the Wine Trail through Biblical Times

Jesus among the Vines

"They have no wine.... Do whatever he tells you" (John 2:3, 5).
—Mary, the mother of Jesus, at the wedding feast in Cana

In the gospel of John, Jesus' public ministry begins when Jesus, his mother, Mary, and his disciples attend a Jewish wedding in a small town called Cana. Feasts and celebrations were an important part of the religious and cultural context in which Jesus grew up, so perhaps it is not surprising that Jesus' first miracle happened at such a festivity. It was Jesus' mother who noticed that the hosts had run out of wine and saw the need. Mary encouraged Jesus to step in and save the day, expectant that he would be able to intervene. Jesus, by turning water into wine, made up for what was lacking, turned scarcity into abundance, and protected the host from embarrassment and shame. This story is familiar and beloved to many within the church. What we often don't think about is how important the food and the wine were in creating such joyous occasions. We often don't think that wine, in addition to being the primary drink at the time, also had significant spiritual meaning.

Have you ever wondered what Jesus, his family, and his followers would drink? Given Mary's great concern about the lack of wine at the wedding, perhaps she was involved in growing vines and making wine for her own meals and family celebrations. Would Jesus and his family have been treading grapes in the community winepress just outside of Nazareth, the one that you can still see today? Would they have had a cellar beneath their house with leather skins full of wine stacked away in the dark and cool? Jesus' familiarity with wineskins (Matt. 9:17; Mark 2:22; Luke 5:37–38) certainly suggests so. What would their family celebrations have been like? And do these seemingly quotidian details of Jesus' life tell us something about God and our relationship with him?

Stepping back into biblical times takes an act of the imagination. Most of us are so far removed from the world of the Bible and the agrarian life that it represents. It is hard to envision the farms and fruit orchards, the village wells and sheep herds, the olive groves and vineyards that Jesus would have walked by every day. Most of us live in cities and suburban neighborhoods, fenced in by garage doors and streets made of asphalt, surrounded by shopping malls, grocery stores, and golf courses. We hop into our cars and watch the world race by from the confines of our car windows, never smelling the manure on the fields and the fermenting fruit wafting from the cellars below. Jesus' life was vastly different from ours.

Jesus grew up in Nazareth, a village nestled in the fertile hill country of southern Galilee, with wonderful views of the surrounding countryside and the Sea of Galilee below in the far distance, about fifteen miles to the east. It was an agrarian community, and most villagers, including Mary and Joseph, would have grown at least some of their own food and made their own small batches of wine. The remnants of thousands of winepresses all over Canaan attest to the widespread production of wine to serve the daily needs of its inhabitants.[1] You might be surprised to read that wine became the primary drink of the Israelites. In places where fresh and clean water was at times scarce and the risk of contamination real, wine became an important source of safe fluids that could be stored in wineskins and sealed stone vessels for long periods of time.

First-century Jewish historian Josephus, a near contemporary of Jesus, tells us that the people of Galilee cultivated every inch of their soil and grew all kinds of lovely and edible things there. Olive groves, pomegranate trees, and vines grew along the surrounding hills and terraces, sprawling down into the valleys below.[2] Jesus and his family would have eaten olives, fresh bread dipped in olive oil, and vinegar, honey, lamb meat, fish from the Sea of Galilee— and yes, they would have enjoyed wine on a regular basis, like most Jewish families at that time.

Wine was a staple in their diet and a safe source of liquid because the alcohol in the wine would have killed most bacteria. Water wasn't always safe to drink, and the danger of water contamination was a very real threat. The global pandemic of COVID-19 gave the twenty-first-century world a new awareness of how important it must have been back then to keep things clean and sanitized. Wine wasn't just drunk to quench one's thirst safely and to enhance celebrations. It was also used to disinfect wounds (think of the parable of the Good Samaritan in Luke 10:25–37) and as a general healing agent (think of Timothy's stomachaches in 1 Tim. 5:23). In those times wine was a multipurpose remedy.

It's hard for us to imagine this. We think of wine as something we enjoy with a nice meal cooked at home or when going out for a special dinner at a restaurant. We might still wonder whether we should or want to drink wine at all. But Jesus grew up in a time and culture where growing vines and crafting wine was one of the major industries in Galilee and in Jewish culture. It was an all-prevalent reality seeping into every aspect of life: the home, the garden, the marketplace, family and village celebrations small and great, and— perhaps most important—worship at the temple and religious practices. Crafting wine was an ancient tradition that the Jewish people inherited from the Canaanites. The world's oldest and largest wine cellar belonging to a royal Canaanite palace was found in Tel Kabri, a day's walk from where Jesus grew up.[3] The wines of Canaan were so famous that the upper class of Egypt imported them into their royal wine cellars. The Son of God grew up in a famous wine region. Who would have thought?

I often wonder what kind of wine they would have made in the first century. Certainly a range of red wines, but perhaps those cooler climates of the elevated hillsides would also have been good for growing certain white wine varieties. Pliny the Elder, a first-century Roman naturalist, devoted a whole volume to wine and mentions nearly two hundred grape varieties, mostly reds, but also some whites.[4] The vines growing along the rocky hillsides made primarily of limestone would have been more stressed than vines growing on flat land within easier reach of water. Some say that makes for a better vintage. We do know that the good water drainage of the hillsides, the higher elevation, the cooler climate, and the longer sun exposure surely would have contributed to a later harvest and a more interesting vintage, probably more complex than those wines from the valleys where the blazing sun would have driven lots of sweetness into the grapes but perhaps less variation and complexity.

Though Jesus is seemingly hesitant to make this wedding the beginning of his public ministry, he gives in to his mother's persistent pleas and moves to action. He directs the servants to fill six large stone jars with water, jars usually reserved for rites of purification customary at the time. Somewhere in between the jars being filled with water and the servants bringing a sample of the "water" to the sommelier at the wedding, the water becomes wine, miraculously. Scarcity is turned into an abundance of choice wine. The wine in those six stone jars would have amounted to somewhere between 640 to 960 bottles of excellent wine.

It is a lavish and quiet miracle. Only a few even notice it—maybe just Jesus' mother, Mary, the servants, and the disciples. The sommelier at the wedding tastes the wine and exclaims in astonishment, "Everyone serves the good wine first and then the inferior wine after the guests have become drunk. But you have kept the good wine until now" (John 2:10). He does not seem to have noticed that the host had run out of wine and is puzzled. It's counter to common sense to bring out the best wine last when people don't pay attention to the quality anymore. Perhaps he never learned of the miraculous provision of wine. Mary, some of the servants, and Jesus' disciples were "in the know," but they might never have made it public because this would have brought great shame and embarrassment to the host, who should not have run out of wine in the first place.

The wedding feast of Cana happened not too far from where Jesus grew up, and the sommelier would have known how to distinguish between a choice wine and a mediocre wine. Growing up and living in a famous wine region, quite a few of the Jews of Jesus' time would have known how to distinguish a good wine from a bad one. But their talk about wine would have been nothing like the kind of wine talk we hear today. They would have talked about where the wine was from, perhaps the vintage and what was added to the wine (herbs, grape must, honey, etc.). They might have remembered the harvest of that particular year and who was involved in treading the grapes and making it.

Today, because most of us have no connection to the places and the people who make wine, wine writers and wine critics have taken that place in society, and they have made it their job to enlighten us and help us connect with the wine and where it came from. While that comes in handy if you are a wine enthusiast, for the ordinary wine drinker this can quickly become intimidating, daunting, and patronizing. Too many still think that wine is an elitist drink reserved for the well-to-do and educated.[5] Who can remember the names of all those grape varieties and exotic and hard-to-pronounce places in France, Italy, and New Zealand? I hope you will be relieved to know that this kind of talk about wine hasn't been around for too long: perhaps fifty years or so. Before wine globalization, most folks would have enjoyed their local wines and focused more on how the wine helped with their conversations, convivial celebrations, and creativity, knowing that a good wine can lift a simple meal to another sphere and strengthen the bonds of kinship and community.

Certainly Jesus wasn't an elitist snob, creating an atmosphere of superiority around his miracle-working wine soiree. On the contrary, he remained in the background, diverting attention away from himself. He loved the people around him and wanted to deepen their sense of joy and convivial celebration. He stepped back so that the gifts of God could touch people's lives and lift their spirits up to their benevolent creator.

In Jesus' time, wine was first of all a spiritual reality: a gift from God, grown on God's promised land and sacred soil, made to grow by God himself, who causes the sun to shine, rain to fall, and plants to grow (Psalm 104; Job 36:27–33). The harvest would have been a religious event with prayers and blessings said and the drinking of wine and the eating of food a sacred act done with due reverence and gratitude. The farmers would have proudly brought an offering of the first vintage of the year to the temple just as God commanded in Leviticus 23. Offering up the firstfruits to God was how they remembered over and over again that all that the earth brings forth is a gift from God and has spiritual meaning. What wisdom lay in these temple rituals that we so often look down on as archaic remnants of the past.

Just outside the town of Nazareth, you can still visit the grape-processing facility hewn into rock that they would have used to crush the grapes with their feet. Have you ever imagined Jesus stomping grapes, cheering and celebrating with his family, relatives, friends, and townspeople, and giving thanks to God for a successful harvest?

After crushing the grapes, they would have gathered up the grape juice as it flowed down from the main basin into the lower basin. Perhaps Jesus' family used wineskins rather than stone vessels to collect the grape juice, since Jesus was so familiar with them and how they were used. In Jesus' teaching, these wineskins become holy ground for exploring the dynamics of the kingdom of heaven (Matt. 9:17).

In Jesus' time, the grape harvest season would have been a community affair. Once the grapes are ripe, it is important to harvest them quickly to keep the sugar content and acidity nicely balanced and to make sure the grapes are processed as quickly as possible. Every hand available in the town would have been called upon. I can't help but think that Jesus would have walked by the vines often and tasted the grapes to see whether they were ripe yet. My grandfather always chided me and told me not to eat the sour grapes. But when no one was looking, I would still eat them because it took so long for the grapes to ripen and I found it hard to wait, watching them ripen so slowly on the vine every day. Farmers and vintners have to learn to be patient. You can't tell grapes to hurry up. They ripen at their leisure. You have to adapt your life to their rhythm, and that takes humility and patience. But once the grapes are ripe and the harvest is ready, there is great commotion, joy, and celebration. Together, Jesus' community would have harvested the grapes and then joined in to give thanks for a successful harvest, renewing their faith and hope in their benevolent creator, being amazed at all that this earth brings forth.

When we think about "what would Jesus drink?" we are taken into a world that beckons us to a life in a close-knit community. They were a people who saw themselves as God's chosen people before they saw themselves as individual believers. It is hard for us to imagine how they would have understood themselves. We live in a time when for generations we have been taught to think of ourselves as individuals long before we think of ourselves as members of a community. In church we are taught to remember our baptism, but are we also taught to remember that we were baptized into a new *family*, a family that now becomes the primary place where we live out our salvation?

Today, many Christians who want to grow in the spiritual life look for interesting books that might help them. Too often, though, these books are written by writers who see themselves first of all as individuals, and they reflect mostly on their individual lives from this individualistic perspective, addressing you, the reader, as an individual and how you can grow as an individual. It is a self-fulfilling prophecy. It pushes us all deeper and deeper into the mud of Western individualism, which has very little in common with the lives of first-century Christians. This way of thinking makes reading the Bible incredibly difficult because the Bible is not addressed to individuals. The Bible is addressed to a communal body and understands the spiritual life first of all as a communal reality before addressing us as persons within that community. The Bible sometimes refers to this community as "the body of Christ," a potent metaphor that underscores the tight-knit and interdependent community that we Christians are called into. (See for example 1 Corinthians 12.)

In Jesus' time people had a collective identity. They understood themselves to be wedded to their God as a people through the covenant that God had made with them. As a community they longingly waited for God to act. Meanwhile they lived as God's people on the land God had given them, drawing on the wisdom of their ancestors in knowing how to work the land, harvest it, and share the harvest with those in need. The Bible taught them how to live as God's people in God's land and to be a blessing to those around them.

When Jesus called his disciples to follow him, the first thing he did was to take them to a family wedding in Cana. And when he performed his first miracle of turning water into wine, he revealed in a glorious way that in him, God's promises of old are being fulfilled. The abundance of wine hints at the abundance of life that God wants to impart to his followers. And into this abundance we are invited. Wine both hints at this abundant life and becomes one way we can experience it.

This book invites you, through the lens of wine, to imagine the world from which Jesus came, what it meant for Jesus' community to be the people of God, and how this vision continued to inspire the church and its communal practices throughout the ages. This book will beckon you to ask how you can grow into this kind of communal life even as you live in places that seem diametrically opposed to the agrarian, communal, and religious life of first-century Palestine. Jesus was accused of being a winebibber (Matt. 11:19; Luke 7:34). Table fellowship, sharing food, and drinking wine together was an integral part of how he ushered in the kingdom of God, how he brought heaven down to earth, and how he challenged the status quo. Jesus loved dinner parties, especially those that included people who were on the fringe. He was a friend of sinners and social outcasts and loved them unconditionally. He did so by breaking all cultural and religious rules and unashamedly and freely sharing food, wine, and table fellowship with them. This radical action of acceptance transformed their lives (Matt. 11:19). Beware, this book might make you into something similar.

2

Beginnings

Covenants, Blessings, and Promises

"May God give you of the dew of heaven and of the fatness
of the earth and plenty of grain and wine" (Gen. 27:28).
—Isaac blessing Jacob, his son

When you eat from a vine, it is tempting to think that the vine produces the grapes and forget that there is a whole root system beneath the surface that supports, nourishes, and sustains the vine and the grapes. In the same way, when you want to learn about Jesus, it is tempting to begin in the New Testament and just stay there. However, if you really want to understand Jesus, then you will have to read everything about him in light of the Hebrew Scriptures, or what Christians call the Old Testament. The New Testament is the vine, the branches, and the grapes, and the Hebrew Scriptures are the rootstock of the New Testament. Without understanding this root system, Jesus easily becomes a free-floating idea and isn't grounded in the history of his own making. The Bible that Jesus and his followers read were the Hebrew Scriptures, and Jesus referred to them often and reinterpreted them in light of his own life and ministry.

The theme of wine is no exception, and it is a fascinating journey to see how this theme unfolds in the Bible and climaxes in Jesus' life and ministry. You might be surprised to find out that food features quite prominently in the Bible and that wine is the most talked about biblical food of all. Wine is mentioned more than bread, olive oil, lamb meat, or fish. There are nearly a thousand references to wine and wine related themes in the Bible: in the New Testament there are around 170 occurrences, while the Old Testament features 810.[1] Whenever the theme of wine comes up in the New Testament, it usually builds upon themes in the Hebrew Scriptures and develops them in new and often surprising ways.

For example, when Jesus performs his first miracle of turning water into wine at the wedding feast of Cana, he fulfills the promises of old—but not quite in the way God's people had envisioned it. He does not fuel or meet the expectation that he might use his divine power and influence to overthrow the Romans and deliver God's people from their oppressors by force. Instead, as we shall see later, Jesus ushers in God's kingdom in an altogether different kind of way. For now, I want us to understand the rootstock from which Jesus emerged.

Beginnings

The theme of wine in the Bible begins when God makes a covenant with Noah after the flood and Noah proceeds from this monumental experience by planting a vineyard (Genesis 8–9). Noah is the first person in the Bible to become a vintner. Like Adam, he is called a man of the soil. Unlike his ancestors, who planted grains to provide for the necessities of life (Gen. 3:17–19), Noah advances to a higher form of agriculture and crafts wine.

In the ancient Near East, wine was a highly esteemed cultural good that not only laid the foundation for feasts and celebrations but also played an important role in shaping civilizations and forming the high cultures within them. The "Standard of Ur" wooden box (approx. 2500 BCE), which is held at the British Museum in London, depicts banqueting scenes of Sumerian society and gives witness to this rich tradition, revealing wine's role in these high cultures.[2]

Noah's father, Lamech, prophetically names his son "Noah," which means "rest," because he is to bring relief and comfort to his people: "Out of the ground that the Lord has cursed this one shall bring us relief from our work and from the toil of our hands" (Gen. 5:29). This promise seems to come to fruition when Noah takes up the vocation of a vintner and crafts wine for his family. In the agrarian societies of the ancient Near East, working the land and growing one's own food was very hard manual labor with few comforts to be had. For us who live in urban contexts, work at computers, and pick up food and wine easily from grocery stores or at restaurants, it is difficult even to imagine what their daily lives were like.

To cook a meal, they had to draw water from a well nearby. They had to grow and harvest vegetables and grains and mill flour for making bread. They kept animals that they milked every day and they made their own cheese. All of this was time-consuming manual labor, and a harvest could easily be wiped out by a natural disaster.

Life was harsh and the culture in which Noah grew up was hostile, evil, and violent to the core (Genesis 6). That is why God decided to wipe the slate clean and allow a flood to destroy humanity: all but Noah and his family and the animals on the ark survived because Noah was different. He walked with God and in the ways of God. He trusted in God and did not give in to the pressures of the surrounding culture. He remained faithful and listened to God. By faith he built an ark—which must have taken years—without any waters in sight. Noah was prepared when disaster struck. He was a remarkable man of faith.

After the flood receded, God commanded Noah to leave the ark, settle down with his family and livestock, and be fruitful and multiply. He is like a second Adam. Noah continued to trust in God. The first thing he did upon leaving the ark was to make an altar to worship God and offer animal sacrifices. He gave back to God what belonged to God in the first place. His animal flock must have been greatly decimated after the flood, and Noah's willingness to give up more of them revealed his unfaltering belief in God's faithfulness and provision. Noah envisioned a hopeful future pregnant with divine possibilities. He remained a man of faith.

The next thing we learn about Noah is that he planted a vineyard. This planting is also an act of faith. Noah believed that God had big plans for his people, and he got to play a small part in these plans. Planting a vineyard was an act of faith in God's future. Nothing in Noah's life indicated that his descendants would one day become a civilization in one of the most conducive areas for vineyards and winemaking on the Fertile Crescent, where the first civilizations of human history emerged. This promise God made to Abram (later called Abraham), one of Noah's descendants (Gen. 15:5–6, 17–21). What God did promise to Noah, however, was foundational for a new civilization to emerge: that he would uphold creation and its fruitfulness (Gen. 8:22). By faith Noah planted a vineyard and invested in the long-term future of God's people. It was a remarkable act of faith.

Covenant and Wine

In between these two acts of building an altar for worship and planting a vineyard, God makes a covenant with Noah and all the living creatures that survived the flood (Gen. 9:9–11). In this covenant God orders creation anew and gives Noah an important role in it. As a man of the earth, he is called to multiply and populate it. This covenant with Noah is built upon God's promise that he will sustain creation and its fruitfulness: "As long as the earth endures, seedtime and harvest . . . shall not cease" (Gen. 8:22). Noah now has a vocation, and God promises that he will provide what is necessary for Noah to fulfill his part of the covenant.

The context of the covenant is important. A covenant is a binding and lasting commitment that God makes with his people. God makes a covenant with Noah, Abraham, Moses, and David.

Jesus makes a new covenant with his followers at the Last Supper. Covenants are the defining ways by which God makes us a people and invites us into relationship with him, a relationship that is rooted in God's eternal faithfulness.

In the ancient Near East, covenant-making was often done in the context of partaking of bread and wine and anointing of oil as symbolic acts, sealing the making of covenants. Reality was recreated and ordered anew in the making of these covenants, which were followed by feasts to "seal the deal."

I find it quite striking that after the making of this covenant between God and Noah, the first thing we learn of Noah is that he plants a vineyard. Why plant a vineyard that will not bear fruit for many years?

Noah reminds me of the wise and industrious woman in Proverbs 31, who buys a field and plants a vineyard, investing in the long-term future and well-being of her family. Of all the crops that the wise woman could have planted, it is the vineyard she chooses.

To me this is a remarkable act of faith in God and God's future. As someone who grew up on a winery, I have always wondered why Noah would begin his new life by planting a vineyard. Why did he not begin by growing grains like his ancestors did, a fast yielding crop to provide for the necessities of daily life quickly? It takes four to five years for a vineyard to grow and bear fruit, but once it is established, it can bear fruit for a lifetime, forty to fifty years and more.

Noah, like the wise woman in Proverbs, hopes in the future and trusts in God. He fulfills his part of the covenant by being a man of the earth: he tends to the soil and plants a vineyard. It is quite striking to me that one of the most ancient wine cellars of the world was found near the mountain range of Ararat, where Noah's ark landed, in modern-day Areni, Armenia. It is said to be more than six thousand years old.[3]

Noah, not having had any experience with alcohol, doesn't handle the drinking of wine well and gets drunk: "He drank some of the wine and became drunk" (Gen. 9:21).[4] In this brief account, Noah is not judged for getting drunk. He, like all people and cultures, has to learn how to handle alcohol and to drink wine wisely.

In Proverbs we see how the Hebrew tradition has evolved and gathered up wisdom for how to enjoy wine wisely (Prov. 9:2, 5; 20:1; 23:20–21, 31–35; 31:4–7).[5] These lessons in Proverbs serve as the prelude to the wise woman who plants her vineyard (Prov. 31:16) and handles its fruit with wisdom.

> In 2010, archaeologists announced the discovery of one of the oldest wineries of the world, called "Areni-1," named after the village where it was found. Areni is located near the mountains of Ararat, where according to Genesis, Noah's ark landed (Gen. 8:4).

Noah's youngest son, Ham, and Ham's son Canaan, are severely judged for Ham's action:[6] he finds his drunk father naked and asleep in his tent, and instead of covering him up and protecting his honor and reputation, he gossips about it and intensifies the shame his father and his family will experience once the news has spread. He disrespects his father and taints Noah's reputation even to the biblical interpreters of today who describe Noah's "downfall" from being a man of God to becoming a drunkard. But wait a minute! This is a harsh judgment and in no way indicated by the biblical text. Did not even Jesus imbibe wine, leading some of his fellow Jews to call him a drunkard (Matt. 11:19; Luke 7:34)?

We are not told what Noah uses the wine for, whether it was just for communal celebrations, for the sealing of covenants he might make with others, or as a sacrificial offering to God. It is only after the exodus that God commands his people to bring wine as a sacrificial offering (Ex. 29:40; Num. 15:5, 7, 10; 18:12; 28:14).

Blessings and Wine

What we do learn from the psalmist, who retells the story of creation in Psalm 104, is that wine is a gift from God, is part of his good creation, and has a particular mission in our lives: "You [God] . . . bring forth food from the earth and wine to gladden the human heart"

(Ps. 104:14–15). Wine isn't meant to bring only comfort, it is meant to bring us joy and enhance our feasts and celebrations. God desires for his people to flourish and to find joy in this life here on earth. As God redeems his beloved creation (Psalm 103), he will continue to allow his beautiful and bountiful world to flourish. In Psalm 104, wine now becomes part of Eden redeemed and has an important role to play.[7]

When I first came across this passage, it made complete sense to me, having grown up on a winery. Though our lives on the winery were incredibly hard, as making a living off the soil will always be, the enjoyment of the fruit of our labor was all the more beautiful and enjoyable because of all the work that had gone into it. But you might find the psalmist's unashamed affirmation of wine unsettling, especially if you come from a family with a history of alcohol abuse that has suffered tremendous pain because of it. It might seem unfathomable that God could use wine to bring comfort and joy to his people.

From the time of Noah, vineyards, vines, and wine become a regular feature in God's story with his people. Abraham gets to enjoy wine at the table of King Melchizedek (Gen. 14:18). His son Isaac elevates wine to new heights that fundamentally shaped the vision of God's people for the future. He blesses his son Jacob to carry on the covenant between God and his people, and part of this blessing comes in the form of, yes, wine. This is so important that the Bible carefully records the words of this blessing that Isaac speaks over his son Jacob: "May God give you of the dew of heaven and of the fatness of the earth and plenty of grain and wine" (Gen. 27:28). It is an iconic moment in the formation of God's people, and this particular blessing looms large in the imagination of God's people as they anticipate God's promises.

Jacob continues this tradition when he blesses his son Judah but lifts it to unprecedented heights when his blessing takes on extravagant dimensions for an abundance of wine in Judah's future: "The scepter will not depart from Judah. . . . He will tether his donkey to a vine, his colt to the choicest branch; he will wash his garments in wine, his robes in the blood of grapes" (Gen. 49:10–12 NIV).

This blessing is a vision not of a skimpy vineyard with a few humble vines but of a massive planting where the vines can grow like trees and produce a great abundance of wine. It is as if Jacob is reenvisioning the garden of Eden on earth as a lush and fruit-laden vineyard where God and his people can live in peace and enjoy the bounty of God's good creation. What a blessing to speak, and what longing it must have stirred in God's people. Surely such grandiose vineyards could not flourish in Egypt, where the blessing was spoken. There must be another place where such bounty could be found!

Promises and Wine

Before Jacob spoke this blessing over Judah, he had followed his son Joseph to Egypt, where Joseph had become a successful and influential statesman. After Joseph's death, however, and over time, things became difficult for his descendants in Egypt. As they increased in numbers and as the memory of Joseph waned, the Israelites began to be oppressed and became slaves in Egypt.

But God hadn't forgotten about them or his covenant with them. He sees the plight of his chosen people and promises to deliver them out of bondage in Egypt. He begins to speak to his people about taking them to a "good and spacious land, to a land flowing with milk and honey" (Ex. 3:8). It is the very land that God had promised to Abraham, Isaac, and Jacob (Ex. 6:8; 33:1). Surely the blessings that both Isaac and Jacob spoke over their sons loom large in the imagination of their descendants as the enslaved Israelites ponder the hope of deliverance and the promise of their very own land.

This place will come into focus after the exodus, when the Israelites first arrive at the borders of the land that God had promised to them, the land of Canaan. God instructs Moses to send spies into the land. Moses tells his spies to check out the land. How strong is the enemy? How rich is the land agriculturally? Is the soil fruitful? Do trees grow there? (Num. 13:17–20). The narrator tells us that all this happened during harvest time, "the season of the first ripe grapes" (v. 20). This brief and seemingly insignificant note reveals how important the grape harvest and the production of wine must have been in the imagination of the Israelites. Hadn't God promised that he would send them to a land with bountiful vineyards? Harvest time seems like a great time to check out how fruitful the land would be and whether it would measure up to the promises that God had made.

The spies, leaders from each of the twelve tribes, search out the land until they come upon a valley where they find vines with massive grape clusters on them. It took two spies to carry just one grape cluster on a pole between them, so large and heavy was this single cluster of grapes that they harvested. The vine itself must have been like a tree to hold up such massive grape clusters. They name this valley Wadi Eschol (Hebrew for the "valley of grape cluster") after the grape cluster they find there.

Have you ever made the connection that one of those spies would have been from the tribe of Judah, a descendant of Judah himself, over whom Jacob spoke this lavish and colorful blessing we mentioned earlier? Jacob spoke of massive vines to which one could tie a donkey and a grape harvest that would produce wine in great excess, evoking images of paradisiacal splendor. What would those spies have felt when they saw that Jacob's vision could become reality?

The prophetic blessings Isaac spoke over Jacob and Jacob spoke over Judah finally seemed within reach. However, the spies were terrified of the enemies in the land and painted a gloomy picture of it as they reported back to the Israelites. It would be another forty years of wandering in the wilderness before they ventured into the land that God had promised them. The promises of God kept them going on this long and arduous journey, promises of a fruitful land that they could call home one day, with an abundance of food that they could grow: wheat and barley, olive oil, and yes, plenty of wine (Deut. 6:10–11; 7:12–13; 8:7–10; 11:14; 33:28).

Are you surprised to learn that God's redemption includes land and soil, fig trees and olives, vineyards, and wine? The so-called Mediterranean triad of grain, wine, and oil is mentioned repeatedly in the Old Testament and is linked to God's promises, blessings, and redemption. The abundance of the earth speaks of the abundance of our God, and he makes himself known through the agricultural gifts that he gives to us. Are you someone who, like me, thought that a blessing from God is a kind of immaterial bond between God and us where we experience his goodness, somehow?

In the Hebrew Scriptures, God's relationship with his people was woven through their connection with the land that they cultivated, and every harvest was a sure sign that God had blessed them. This is the world in which Jesus grew up and affirmed as his own.

Perhaps it is tempting to think that this was an Old Testament reality but that in the New Testament things are different. Land doesn't seem to feature much anymore, nor does the agricultural world of the Hebrew Scriptures. Didn't Jesus leave his father's trade as a carpenter and did not some of his followers leave the world of fishing to become fishers of men? Isn't Jesus more concerned with the heart and spiritual matters than with things of this world?

We have to remember that Jesus takes the place of the priestly order (Hebrews 4) and the Jewish rabbis who were the authorities on teaching the Torah (Mark 1:22; 10:51). The priests and rabbis in the Hebrew Scriptures weren't directly involved in agriculture either, but they relied on the farming community to bring agricultural sacrifices for worship and to provide them and their tribes with food so they could perform their God-ordained ministries.

When Jesus established a new covenant with his disciples and instituted the Lord's Supper, he used agricultural products—bread and wine—to make known to his followers the mysteries of his death and resurrection. We approach God through the world that he has made and that he called good. Food and wine remain fundamental to how the New Testament envisions our relationship with Christ. We cannot sidestep the world that God has made to arrive at a purer form of the Christian life. This would be heresy.

This should raise many questions for us. What does the Christian faith, for example, have to do with the freshwater crisis in Jackson, Mississippi, where, during the summer of 2022, residents were without access to safe drinking water? Or the Flint water crisis in Michigan, where contaminated drinking water made residents sick? Or the many food deserts all over America, where residents have few to no options to access affordable and healthy foods such as fresh fruits and vegetables? Is this a spiritual matter? What would Jesus have offered them? Why do so many churches still believe that this isn't any of their business?

The gospel of John in particular reminds us that Jesus is not only our redeemer but also our creator and provider. In the beginning of John's gospel, Jesus is affirmed as the one who was in the beginning and that all things were created through him (John 1:1–3). His first miracle of turning water into wine (John 2), his miraculous feeding of the crowds (John 6), and his cooking breakfast to feed his disciples (John 21) reveal Jesus as Lord over his creation and as the one who provides for us. Ultimately, all things come from Jesus, including water and, yes, wine, the fruit of God's earth and the work of human hands.

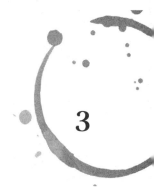

3

Fulfillments

Living into God's Presence

*During Solomon's lifetime Judah and Israel lived in safety, from Dan
even to Beer-sheba, all of them under their vines and fig trees.*
—1 Kings 4:25

Fulfillments

The Israelites do enter and settle in the promised land eventually, and
here they learn to live as God's people in God's land. Moses reminds
them never to forget that it was God who brought them out of Egypt
and into a land of plenty, and always to remember God and his faithfulness toward them. The exodus and the promised land now profoundly shape the identity of God's people: God delivers them out of
bondage in Egypt, and God provides an agriculturally rich land where
they can settle and live as God's people in God's land. By offering up
the firstfruits of each harvest, they acknowledge and remember that
all that this land brings forth is ultimately a gift from God. It is never
to be taken for granted, and it is to be shared with those in need.

The vision in 1 Kings 4:25, harking back to Leviticus, captures in moving ways how God's people were to live in the promised land, a dream come true, at least for a season: "During Solomon's lifetime Judah and Israel lived in safety, from Dan even to Beer-sheba, all of them under their vines and fig trees."[1] It is a beautiful and yet also a humble vision, not of grand and wealthy landowners but of families cultivating their own small farms that produce enough to provide for their daily needs, to share with the poor, and to allow for a little extra for special celebrations. Archaeological evidence of ancient Israel suggests that these small family-owned vineyards produced around 182 gallons or approximately 694 liters of wine per year, amounting to two and a half bottles of wine a day with some extra wine for special occasions.[2] Two and a half bottles of wine per day is a significant amount for a family, but you have to remember that wine was their principal drink because access to safe fresh water was not always available. Wine also had more nutritional value than water and was considered a food staple.[3]

Settling into the promised land and planting vineyards, fig trees, and wheat and allowing each family to enjoy a modest abundance was only part of what God had called the Israelites to do. They also had to learn what it means to be God's people and remain faithful to God and the calling he had placed upon them. In this land, as they were sowing seeds and planting vineyards, raising livestock, and working the olive presses, they learned to be God's people. They learned what it means to love God with their whole being and what it means to love their neighbors as themselves (Deut. 6:4–6; Leviticus 19). They were called to walk in God's ways and keep his commandments and to reflect God's presence in a hostile world where the worship of false gods, violence, injustice, and cruelty were common. God blessed them so they could be a blessing. How they treated those around them mattered, especially those on the margins and without means. The Torah gave them guidelines to live this holy life, a life set apart for God. The book of Leviticus was the road map that guided them in this life. The Israelites were to be like a holy flame shining brightly in the darkness.

Living in God's Presence

The rhythms and rituals that kept the Israelites focused on God and their calling to be God's people in God's land shaped all spheres of life, and wine had an important role to play in most of them. It came to play an important part in Israel's worship as well as their religious festivals and family celebrations.

As part of their worship in the temple, the Israelites offered sacrifices, and only the best agricultural products, including grain and wine, were permitted (Ex. 29:40; Num. 15:5, 7, 10; 18:12; 28:14). These sacrifices had various functions, such as soliciting God's blessing, receiving the forgiveness of sins, purification from ritual impurity, or offering praise and thanksgiving to God for one's life and well-being. The fact that wine became elevated to a sacrificial drink offering reveals how valuable wine had become and how esteemed its role was in the life of Israel and their relationship with God.

Keeping the Sabbath every week and allowing the land to have a whole Sabbath year every seventh year (Lev. 25:1–7) was another way that the Israelites learned to trust in God and his provision. They rested from their daily labor. It was one of the most important commandments: keep the Sabbath holy! (Ex. 20:8; Lev. 23:3). On the Sabbath they worshiped, rested, and enjoyed time with family around the table. They ate freshly harvested food from their farms prepared the day before and savored the latest vintage from their vineyards maturing in wineskins or clay pots in their cool cellars.

Resting takes an act of faith. It is a letting go of one's productivity and achievements and an embrace of the rest that we all long for. God is in charge, and he provides for us. That is a hard lesson to learn. The Sabbath kept the Israelites rooted in this reality: God was their deliverer and provider, and he would continue to provide for them and be with them and near to them. On the Sabbath day, they rested and savored the life that God had given them. Leisurely sipping a little wine as they shared a special meal enhanced this sense of rest and enjoyment of life. The psalmist captures this sense of Sabbath rest most beautifully when he writes, "You show me the path of life. In your presence there is fullness of joy; in your right hand are pleasures forevermore" (Ps. 16:11).

I don't always find it easy to slow down and get the rest I yearn for. My fears, my hidden sense of loneliness and sadness keep me striving and restless even as I long for rest. And then I pick up Wendell Berry's Sabbath poems and a glass of well-crafted wine. The poems paired with the wine remind me that part of our Sabbath is to dare the inner journey through the wilderness of our fears, loneliness, and sadness. I sit with it all for a little while as I sip my wine and learn to be still. And I feel held again in the arms of the living God as I sense his goodness gliding down my tongue, savoring with joy that I have found my eternal home.

God also commanded the Israelites to bring the firstfruits of their harvests as an offering, and that included wine as a drink offering (Ex. 29:38–40; Lev. 23:9–10, 13; Num. 18:27; Deut. 14:22–23; 15:14). It reminded them that though they might own a vineyard and harvest its fruit, ultimately the vineyard belongs to God and the harvest is a rich blessing from God not to be hoarded but enjoyed and shared with those in need. Wine was a highly esteemed cultural good in the ancient Near East, but God made it clear to his people that it was first of all a gift that he gave to *all* of them, not just to the elite as it had been in Egypt.[4]

I remember vividly how my mother would go out into the vineyard in the autumn when the grape clusters had fully ripened. Mom would cut the most beautiful grape clusters from the vines, carefully lay them in a basket, and bring them to our little Lutheran church, nestled in the heart of our medieval village, its steeple unashamedly pointing heavenward. There she would go to the altar and use the grape clusters with their branches to decorate it for our annual harvest thanksgiving service. It was one of those moments when *I learned* that our lives and all we do on the winery belong to God, and in this simple ritual, Mom helped me to orient my life back toward him. I did not know it back then, but my mother was bringing the firstfruits of the harvest to the altar of God.

Many churches don't celebrate a harvest thanksgiving service anymore, and it seems as if agriculture is no longer part of God's domain. Lutheran and Catholic churches in Germany still celebrate it, and it is usually held on the first Sunday of October, right around harvest time. Instead, in our globalized cultures, we have handed over the sacred work of agriculture to the corporate world, whose CEOs would shake their heads at the idea of offering up firstfruits in harvest thanksgiving services, let alone the idea of allowing a plot of land to rest for a whole year. Perhaps when we look at how agriculture is done in our lands, we can realize how secular our own cultures have become not just recently but over the last century.

The forgotten harvest thanksgiving service is perhaps a silent sign of a greater loss in our communities: that we have lost our connection with the land and the living soil, and no longer grow at least some of our own food in our gardens and back yards. Until very recently, families and local family farmers used to grow much of the food for our communities, and they did so in sustainable ways. Through this communal effort, people kept an existential connection with the land through the locally grown food they ate and drank. It rooted them on the land and in relationship with those who grew the food and helped them understand how important agriculture is as a spiritual, cultural, and economic foundation to their lives.[5]

Only the last two or three generations have turned away from gardening and farming. Because politicians decided to favor and support agribusinesses, large corporations now grow much of our food, and they care little about God, the health of the land, or the well-being of the people who live on this land. Most foods grown, harvested, and processed by these agribusinesses are processed into unhealthy foods. They create an unbalanced diet and contribute to now common diseases such as type-2 diabetes, various types of cancer, Alzheimer's, and cardiovascular diseases, to name just a few. It is a desecrated world where traces of the divine are as barren as the soil leached of its natural organic life because of intensive farming practices.

Sustainable agriculture is not a romantic relationship with nature. It is a relationship of labor and toil, miraculous growth as seeds fall into the ground and abundant crops rise into the heavens, as grape leaves gather the sunrays and ripen the grape clusters to sweet fruition through photosynthesis. It is an awe-inspiring work that grounds communities and naturally lifts their hearts to the heavens, where God sends forth rain to water the earth. Leviticus puts this agrarian vision, addressed to future family farmers, beautifully: "If you follow my statutes and keep my commandments and observe them faithfully, I will give you your rains in their season, and the land shall yield its produce, and the trees of the field shall yield their fruit. Your threshing shall overtake the vintage, and the vintage shall overtake the sowing; you shall eat your bread to the full and live securely in your land. And I will grant peace in the land, and you shall lie down, and no one shall make you afraid" (Lev. 26:3–6 NRSV 1995).

This moving poetic vision speaks of God's faithfulness and generosity, the abundance the earth is capable of bringing forth, and the flourishing of all of God's creation.

And yet countries and their sponsored corporations in the twentieth century have set in motion a model that has created scarcity: the loss of fertile topsoil in which we can grow food, the lack of healthy and nutritious food, which in turn has led to the loss of human health.[6] Perhaps most profound, it has led to the loss of any connection that we might experience through working the land and eating fresh, healthy, and flavorful food that not only nourishes our bodies but also delights our souls. The enjoyment of delicious food and fragrant wine can lift our spirits to the heavens with a sense of awe and wonder for what God's earth is capable of bringing forth. So much of this is lost as we open cardboard boxes and remove plastic wrappings from processed food that is overly salty or sugary, covering up for the lack of natural flavor and poor nutritional value. The bounty that the earth is capable of bringing forth is eclipsed, and so is our sense of wonder and awe for what God has made.

Feasts were another way that the Israelites oriented themselves to God and learned that all of life was sacred and a gift from God. This holy life lived in God's presence was to flow over into all spheres of life, including joyous celebrations and extended feasting. Did you know that during Jesus' time, over the duration of the Passover meal, each guest consumed four cups of wine as they retold the story of God's deliverance out of Egypt and cultivated expectant hope for the future?[7]

To celebrate meant to gather, enjoy food and wine, tell stories, dance, and be merry. Wine, together with music and dancing, helped create a festive atmosphere and elicit joy and conviviality. It lifted the guests out of the humdrum of everyday life and all the hardships that went with it into a sense of joyous gratitude for what God had done and would do in the future. The Israelites had feasts that spoke to their lives as farmers and vintners. They had a celebration for the grape harvest, often referred to as the vintage feast, and a feast to celebrate the sheepshearing season. The Jewish vintage feast continues to inspire harvest celebrations in traditional wine-growing regions in France and Germany to this day.[8]

Family celebrations included the weaning of a child (Gen. 21:8), marriage feasts (Gen. 29:21–22), birthdays (Gen. 40:20), the making of covenants (2 Sam. 3:20–21), and the enthronements of kings (1 Chron. 12:40). Jewish wedding feasts were exceptionally elaborate and long-lasting affairs. During the time of Jesus, they lasted up to seven days. Can you imagine a wedding celebration lasting a whole week? No wonder that Jesus transformed such a massive amount of water into an abundance of wine at the wedding feast of Cana, given that the guests might stick around for a whole week. And perhaps it is not so surprising anymore that a bridegroom could run out of wine at his own wedding!

The Passover Feast was also a great and prolonged celebration. As the Israelites went on pilgrimage to Jerusalem with songs of deliverance on their lips, they gathered to celebrate this monumental event of salvation. They remembered that God delivered them and brought them to a fertile land where they could flourish as a people and cultivate vineyards and craft their own vintages. Psalm 126, rich with agricultural metaphors, meditates on God's redemptive work in their midst: "When the LORD restored the fortunes of Zion, we were like those who dream. Then our mouth was filled with laughter, and our tongue with shouts of joy. . . . Restore our fortunes, O LORD, like the watercourses in the Negeb. May those who sow in tears reap with shouts of joy. Those who go out weeping, bearing the seed for sowing, shall come home with shouts of joy, carrying their sheaves" (Ps. 126:1–2, 4–6).

Just like the farmer harvests fruit from the land, so do the Israelites harvest joy as they remember and ponder God's deliverance. Joy is the harvest of the faithful who cultivate in their midst the remembrance of what God has done. And wine has an important role to play in this harvest of joy: God gave wine "to gladden the human heart" (Ps. 104:15). The psalmist singles out wine as a gift from God that will elicit and deepen this sense of joy. It is a beautiful vision that embeds the gift of wine in God's desire to set his people free and allow them to live joyfully in his presence as they savor the fruits of the land that God had given to them.[9]

4

Mission Failed, God's Judgment, and Renewed Promise

Mission Failed

God's people were richly blessed in the promised land and the paradisiacal overtones can hardly be missed. But that blessing was not an end in itself. Just as God had called Abraham and blessed him so he could be a blessing to the nations (Gen. 12:1–3), so did God call the Israelites and bless them so that they could be a blessing, especially to their neighbors and those who were vulnerable: the poor, the widows, the orphans, and the strangers in the land.

Leviticus 19 is the great code to care for one's community and be a blessing to others. The Israelites are commanded to love their neighbor, and one way to do that is to help feed those who have no means to feed themselves: "You shall not strip your vineyard bare or gather the fallen grapes of your vineyard; you shall leave them for the poor and the alien: I am the LORD your God" (Lev. 19:10).[1] This command to care for the poor in the Israelites' midst resounds throughout the Scriptures even to the point that Christ identified himself with the hungry (Matt. 25:42).

God's people were not to be a money- and property-hoarding people, adding field to field to amass wealth and power. Instead, they were to be a people in which each family could enjoy a modest abundance and had enough to share with those in need (Isa. 5:8; 1 Kings 4:25). In their agricultural setting, it meant to share the harvest and leave grapes hanging on the vine and sheaves of grain standing in the field. Then strangers like the widow Ruth could find food and survive and perhaps even find her way into becoming part of the faith community (Ruth 2:14–23). Rather than exploiting the poor and taking advantage of them, God's people were called to take care of them. It was a core value that God never wanted them to forget. But eventually they did, and it became their downfall.

Perhaps the most tragic passage in the Bible that speaks of a vineyard is found in the book of Isaiah, when the prophet speaks of God's beloved people as a vineyard. As agrarian people, the Israelites would have been able to relate to the metaphor of the vineyard well, and all sorts of associations would arise in their imagination, such a need to stay rooted in God, their dependence on God the vintner for pruning, watering, and protection, and their calling to become a fruitful nation and a blessing to others.[2]

The haunting love poem about God's vineyard in Isaiah 5, however, is tragic as it laments the once great love affair between God and his people and foretells their dooming fate: "I will sing for my beloved my love song concerning his vineyard: My beloved had a vineyard on a very fertile hill" (Isa. 5:1). The prophet Isaiah talks of a vintner (God) lovingly planting his vineyard (Israel), protecting it, and caring for it. Over time the vineyard had started to produce only bad fruit. Its grapes were sour and the vine had become useless. Instead of justice there was bloodshed, and the poor were oppressed and cried out to their God. Isaiah confronts this injustice with clear and direct words: "Ah, you who join house to house, who add field to field, until there is room for no one but you" (Isa. 5:8 NRSV 1995). God's people had forgotten their mission to show mercy and take care of the poor, and instead greedily amassed wealth and property instead.

The Winepress Is Churning Out God's Judgment

As a consequence, Isaiah predicts God's judgment. The Lord will withdraw his protection from his people, the vineyard will be destroyed, and God's people will be carried into exile (Isa. 5:2–7; see also Joel 1:7; Mark 12:1–9). The prophet Jeremiah puts it succinctly: "Yet I planted you as a choice vine from the purest stock. How then did you degenerate and become a wild vine?" (Jer. 2:21; see also 6:9; Ezek. 15:1–6; 17:1–10; Hos. 10:1–2).

All the Sabbath-keeping, sacrifices, burnt offerings, and feasts had become facades behind which the leaders of Judah and Jerusalem hid their cruelty, injustice, and greed: "It is you who have devoured the vineyard; the spoil of the poor is in your houses. What do you mean by crushing my people, by grinding the face of the poor?" (Isa. 3:14–15; see also Amos 8:4–6).

The hardworking farmers, the poor, the widows, and the orphans were no longer being cared for. Instead, the landholding leaders exploited them. Justice was not done, and God's people had lost their fragrant aroma. The elite had turned their feasting into orgies of drunkenness rather than remembering and honoring their God and what he had done for them (Isa. 5:11–13; see also Hos. 4:10–11).

As God removes his protection from his people and especially the unfaithful leadership, his people are carried into exile and they are a free people no more. It is a great tragedy. The woeful song of Psalm 137 laments it: "How could we sing the LORD's song in a foreign land? If I forget you, O Jerusalem, let my right hand wither!" (Ps. 137:4–5). The harps hang unused in the corner, Jerusalem is destroyed, and the Israelites are overcome with sadness. They find themselves in exile, far removed from their beloved land with a profound longing for home.

But there is hope. Eventually God also judges the nations who oppress his people as they live in exile. The vintner God pulls out his pruning knife to prune (judge) the nations (Isa. 18:4–6). The winepress churns out God's judgment against them, they will be crushed like grapes in the winepress, and one day God's people will return to the promised land (Isa. 63:1–6; Joel 3:13).

It is striking to me that the prophets use the language of agriculture and viticulture to speak prophetically. It is the language of the common people: the farmers, the day laborers, and the poor. It liberates them to think against the oppressive system that they find themselves in. And it is these agrarian metaphors that gather momentum into powerful poetry and proclaim the year of the Lord's favor.

The Promise of God's Redemption

The prophets don't just preach doom and gloom, though their poetic words cut deeply into the systemic injustice and oppression of the time. They also give us glimpses of hope that God has not abandoned his people into exile forever. He is merciful and forgiving and longs to restore his people to life as he intended it, being faithful to God, to the land, and to each other.[3]

Hosea, the Bible's countryside prophet, employs the metaphor of the garden and the vine to speak tenderly to God's people: "I will heal their disloyalty; I will love them freely. . . . They shall again live beneath my shadow; they shall flourish as a garden; they shall blossom like the vine; their fragrance shall be like the wine of Lebanon" (Hos. 14:4, 7; see also Isa. 27:2–6).

What strikes me most about this poetic vision of Israel as a garden and a vine is that they will be replanted on land that belongs to God, and the purpose of the vine is to produce fragrant blossoms. The fragrance they will exude is like a choice wine from Lebanon: it will bring nourishment, joy, and well-being to the *whole* community. The fragrance isn't something they conjure up themselves but comes from the core of who they are as God's people: a planting of the Lord, beloved and well tended by their vintner God, who provides all they need to flourish in his garden (Hos. 14:8).

And how exactly does God do that? He paves the way for them to return to their land, which is really *his* land, and rebuild their cities, and each family will be able to have a small plot of land to plant their own gardens and vineyards again and to be able to enjoy their fruit and even their very own wine (Amos 9:14–15). It sounds as if the prophet Amos wants to start a farm-to-table movement!

And sure enough, the prophet Micah continues in a similar vein: wars will cease, and God's people will turn their swords and spears (weapons of war) into plowshares and pruning hooks (gardening tools) and each family "shall sit under their own vines and under their own fig trees, and no one shall make them afraid" (Mic. 4:3–4).

This beautiful and peaceable vision first given in Leviticus is now evoked once more.[4] There will be no more wars and families will live without fear, and they can till their own soil, grow their own food (or at least some of it), and harvest their own grapes to craft their own family wines. Yes, that is exactly how the prophets envision God's redemption. This vision echoes back to the time when Israel first settled in the promised land. Under Solomon's rule they were able to live in peace and every family had their own plot of land with fig trees and vines, enjoying a modest abundance (1 Kings 4:25).

Are you surprised to find out that planting your own vineyard, tending it, harvesting it, and crafting your own wine could become a sign of God's redemption in your life and community? That is not usually what I hear from the pulpit. What I often hear is how God wants to redeem and heal and comfort our souls and make us into nicer and more caring individuals and get involved in community service and more church programs. Such a vision of the Christian life is too human centered and too focused on the individual.

God's good creation is not a scenic backdrop designed only so humans can take the stage.[5] Creation has a greater purpose than serving our human needs and wants. Not all that God created is made for human benefit. Nor is humanity at the center of it all. God is at the center of the universe, and his creation voices the creator's praise: "Let the heavens be glad, and let the earth rejoice, and let them say among the nations, 'The LORD is king!' Let the sea roar and all that fills it; let the field exult and everything in it. Then shall the trees of the forest sing for joy" (1 Chron. 16:31–33, quoting Ps. 96:10–12).

Though the seas and the trees and the fields don't use words to express their praise, their very existence and abundant fruitfulness point to God. As the trees grow into the heavens and their branches move with the winds, those with the eyes of faith sense the praise that the trees are singing.

The psalmist reminds us that the foundation of creation is God: "From your lofty abode you water the mountains; the earth is satisfied with the fruit of your work" (Ps. 104:13). The prophet Isaiah joins this song of praise when he writes, "The mountains and the hills before you shall burst into song, and all the trees of the field shall clap their hands" (Isa. 55:12). In the Bible, creation's first vocation is to sing praise to its creator, and then, in the care of human hands, creation is to continue to sing this praise, lifting us up to join in continual praise of God.

Sadly, we have come of age in a time when creation is often seen as merely a commodity to serve our human needs and wants. There is little understanding of the earth as a sacred place, a place "charged with the grandeur of God," as Gerard Manley Hopkins put it. As humans we get to be part of this amazing creation, but we are only and always merely members of this community of creation that ultimately belongs to God alone. In this human-centered world where "all is seared with trade; bleared, smeared with toil; and wears man's smudge,"[6] we need to readjust our perspective and arrive at a more humble and caring place. As the earth aches under the burden of human exploitation and pollution, we are called to work toward creation's healing and restoration. Ecospirituality seeks to recover this sense of the sacred in creation and is gaining some attention, often on the margins of the church.[7]

Anthropocentric thinking has a long history, but it sure isn't rooted in the Bible; it's not biblical at all.[8] Ecological destruction is often met with indifference, confusion, or apathy in many churches, and I find this heartwrenching. The biblical account upholds all of creation as God's, and our role as humans, especially as believers, is to honor it, care for it, and work toward its redemption.

When the prophet Jeremiah speaks of God's redemption, he speaks of Israel returning to its land with singing, dancing, merrymaking, and vineyard planting (Jer. 31:4–5, 7). For Jeremiah, God's goodness to his people materializes in a bountiful harvest with an abundance of grain, wine, and oil (Jer. 31:12).[9]

The prophet Isaiah envisions God's redemption as a great feast with choice wine for all people: "On this mountain the LORD of hosts will make for all peoples a feast of rich food, a feast of well-aged wines, of rich food filled with marrow, of well-aged wines strained clear" (Isa. 25:6). The prophet Amos even speaks of a time when "the mountains shall drip sweet wine, and all the hills shall flow with it" (Amos 9:13).[10]

Amos's description might seem a bit over the top, but when you visit Israel today and go into the hill country, you discover the remnants of thousands of winepresses hewn into the rocky hills. Once you see them, Amos's vision does not seem so outlandish. The winepresses were built in such a way that the grape juice flowed down from one basin into the next, making the hills look like overflowing fountains. What a sight it must have been during harvest time.

And Hosea, perhaps the most agrarian prophet of all, goes to new visionary heights when he speaks of God's redemption as a great wedding banquet. God is the bridegroom who woos his unfaithful bride back to him to be his wife. He renews his covenant with Israel, and this covenant is as intimate as marriage itself. And to this wedding feast all living creatures are invited: not only humans but the wild animals, the birds of the air, creeping creatures such as ants, caterpillars, and vineyard snails—you name it: all living creatures are invited to join in (Hos. 2:18–20). It's an inclusive party.

In this renewed covenant, God's people get another chance to learn what it means to be righteous and just and how to live out *hesed*,

a Hebrew word we don't really have a word for in English. It is usually translated as "steadfast love" or "love." It means being loving and
faithful within the covenant that God has made. And this covenant
faithfulness isn't just focused on humans but includes the earth and all
that it brings forth, including grain and wine and oil (Hos. 2:21–23).

Nothing is beyond the reach of God's salvation, and all is to be
brought into this covenant *hesed*, where righteousness and justice kiss,
where there is integrity of belief and action, especially when it comes
to the land and what it so generously gives to us (Ps. 85:10–13).

These visions of grandiose feasts and a great wedding banquet
with choice wine flowing down the hills in exuberant abundance are
striking. Many of these prophetic culinary poems inspire a yearning
for paradise restored. Could the harmonious times of Eden, the garden of delight, be brought back? Could there be a time when God
will be with his people in such intimate ways that they could feast
together, drink wine, be merry, and dance for joy? God's people are
pregnant with expectation as they ponder these words and wait for
God's deliverance.

The Israelites do eventually return to their beloved land, but not
as a free people. Foreign empires continue to occupy them as they try
to carve out an existence under oppressive regimes. How could they
sing, dance, celebrate, and enjoy their feasts when God's deliverance
seemed so far out of reach? Where is the bridegroom wooing back
his bride in the free and festive dance of God's salvation?

5

The Bridegroom Is Here

Let the Feasting Begin

"Everyone serves the good wine first and then the inferior
wine after the guests have become drunk. But you
have kept the good wine until now" (John 2:10).
—Sommelier at the wedding feast of Cana

It is into this pregnant moment of occupied Israel's longings and expectations that Jesus begins his ministry. The words of the prophets had been spoken a long time ago. The world had changed, but a free people they were not—not yet. Would God finally send someone who could free them from their latest oppressor, the Roman Empire? Whom would he send? And how would this deliverance come about? They had so many questions, and there were so many unknowns.

This is when Jesus steps onto the scene. Born in an obscure setting and growing up tucked away in a peasant family (what we would today consider a working-class family), he seems the most unlikely candidate. And then, when he finally steps out into the open, his words and deeds pierce the darkness with puzzling signs of hope.

At a humble peasant wedding in a little town called Cana, away from the hustle and bustle of the big cities and political centers of the time, he does something really strange: he turns water into wine, scarcity into abundance, a looming family disaster into a grandiose culinary celebration for insignificant small-town people of whom we will never hear again. It is the first of many signs that Jesus performs to reveal that God is on the move and that surprises are ahead, glorious and strange.

What kind of deliverance is this? Have you ever wondered why Jesus' first miracle wasn't a healing miracle or feeding the hungry by supernaturally multiplying bread? Why would he waste his time partaking in an elaborate and long-lasting family celebration? Why is he not out there solving the world's problems?

Wait a minute. Did the prophets of old not speak of God's deliverance in this way? Didn't Amos, Hosea, and Isaiah tell of a grand celebration where God would be the host and provide a feast with well-aged wine? As with so many of Jesus' words and deeds, they are weighty, reaching back into the past, and redefining the present and the future with good news. Jesus' words and deeds always seem to have multiple levels of meaning to them. It is easy to rush through the story and miss the wealth of meaning it seeks to convey. Let's go slowly through it again and unpack a bit more the riches found in this first of Jesus' miracles.

The host of the wedding has run out of wine, and Mary, Jesus' mother, is the first to notice. She makes her son aware of it, hoping that he will intervene (John 2:3–5). Perhaps the wedding couple are relatives of hers and she is concerned for them and their reputation, wanting the host and the wider family to avoid the acute embarrassment and shame of running out of wine at the wedding. It also would have put a massive damper on the celebration, one of the most important family celebrations they had, lasting up to seven days.

As we have seen, in the Jewish world that Jesus and his disciples inhabited, feasts and celebrations were important ways families and communities cultivated their spiritual lives. As they ate and drank their wine, they remembered God's deeds of the past, embraced God's faithfulness in the present, and fostered expectant hope for

God's redeeming intervention in the future. Celebrations lifted guests out of the mundane into a realm of awareness that opened them up to God and each other. These feasts were meant to continually form and transform them into who they were as God's people.

A Jewish wedding and the feasting that followed were profoundly spiritual affairs because the *hesed* the couple experienced in their marriage covenant was directly related to God's covenant faithfulness. Just as God was faithful to them in the covenant he had made with his people, so would they be faithful to each other in this marriage covenant. And the wine they drank was a sign of God's blessing upon them and the covenant they made with each other in God's presence. To this day, in the Christian Orthodox tradition in Iraq, it is customary for the bride and groom to drink a cup of wine together directly after the marriage ceremony. It reminds the couple that their marriage is a sacrament of *joy*. When I got married, we wove this ritual into our wedding service because I thought it so beautiful and so true. What riches we have lost in our liturgies.

When Jesus decides to act, he asks the servants to fill with water six stone water jars, which are usually set aside for the Jewish rites of purification. Why would he use vessels set aside for ritual washing and use them for a new purpose?

It seems that Jesus cared more for the host and a successful feast where the guests had a good time than for the religious customs and laws of his own people. Such seemingly minor details might pass us by, but at the time it would have been deeply unsettling. Perhaps it would not be unlike filling a baptismal font in church with water and waiting for Jesus to turn it into wine. As beautiful as the wine miracle is, it is also unsettling, overturning religious customs to make room for new wineskins to hold God's ways.

It is quite striking that we get specific measurements for the stone jars: as we saw, each holds between twenty or thirty gallons (John 2:6), and so six stone jars would make between 650 and 960 bottles of wine. John impresses on us that what is about to happen will be lavish and extravagant!

The servants fill the jars with water up to the very brim. Perhaps they sense that something significant is about to happen. Then Jesus tells them to take some and bring it to the master of the banquet. At some point, the water turns into wine, and when the master of the banquet takes a sip, he is pleasantly surprised. He has no idea that they are running out of wine, and so he turns to the bridegroom in astonishment and exclaims, "Everyone serves the good wine first and then the inferior wine after the guests have become drunk. But you have kept the good wine until now" (John 2:10).

What is so striking about this miracle is that Jesus produces an abundance not only of wine but of beautifully fragrant and delicious wine. The sommelier at the wedding feast is stunned by its beauty and puzzled why they would serve it when everyone is already tipsy and unable to really appreciate it.

Few have appreciated the depth, layers, and beauty of this miracle and how it harkens back to the rootstock of the Old Testament. There is certainly more meaning to it than the sheer delight of culinary joys. From the time of Isaac and Jacob, an abundance of wine demonstrated an abundance of God's blessing. And didn't the prophet Isaiah speak of God's future redemption as an invitation to an abundant feast, free of charge, allowing his people to go forth with joy (Isa. 55:1, 12)?

Perhaps the best interpreter of this miracle that I have come across is Russian novelist and mystic Fyodor Dostoevsky. In his great novel *The Brothers Karamazov*, he reflects on the meaning of the miracle. In the novel, Alyosha wants to become a monk in the Russian Orthodox tradition and follow in the footsteps of his spiritual father, Zosima.[1] But before this, Father Zosima challenges Alyosha not to stay in the monastery but to sojourn into the world and live like Christ among the Russian people. In the chapter "Cana of Galilee," Alyosha returns to the monastery to keep watch by the coffin of his beloved Father Zosima, who holds an icon of his savior in his arms. Alyosha's feelings of sorrow are intermingled with a sweetness and even joy as he sits and prays by the coffin of his beloved teacher. Half in slumber, he hears Father Paissy read from the gospel of John. When he recognizes that the reading is the story of the wedding of Cana, he perks up and listens attentively. Alyosha exclaims, "I love that passage: it's Cana of Galilee, the first miracle.... Ah, that miracle, ah, that lovely miracle! Not grief, but men's joy Christ visited when he worked his first miracle, he helped men's joy.... 'He who loves men, loves their joy.'"[2]

Alyosha marvels at Christ, who came to share in the joys of ordinary people. He remembers that God gave wine to make glad the hearts of humanity and that wine is an expression of God's love.

It is this story of God's overwhelming generosity in providing choice wine at a peasant wedding in Cana that gives Alyosha a renewed vision and hope for God's desire to redeem this world. He now recognizes what his vocation in the world might be. He ponders the choice wine that was kept until last, and with the eyes of faith he begins to understand the deeper meaning of this miracle. Without neglecting or minimizing the literal meaning of this first of Jesus' miracles, Dostoevsky, through the eyes of Alyosha, explores its meaning more fully. This wedding feast and the miraculously provided abundance of choice wine point to the heavenly wedding banquet, during which the wine of salvation will flow in great abundance and make glad the hearts of the people. Alyosha hears Father Zosima speak to him as out of a dream, encouraging him to embrace his vocation in the world: "'We are rejoicing,' ... 'We are drinking new wine, the wine of new and great joy. Begin, my dear, begin, my meek one, to do your work!' ... 'Do not be afraid of him. Awful in his greatness before us, terrible is his loftiness, yet he is boundlessly merciful, he became like us out of love, and he is rejoicing with us, transforming water into wine, that the joy of the guests may not end.'"[3]

Alyosha is filled with dread, but he now understands that in a broken world his vocation is to proclaim God's forgiveness. He has to help the people embrace it so that the wine of salvation can flow freely.

The miraculous provision of wine at Cana captures the wonderful and delicious gift that wine is to humanity as a sign of God's blessing and benevolence, but it also draws our attention to the eschatological wedding feast that has already begun in Jesus. Salvation, like an abundance of choice wine, flows freely to all who are willing to receive it. And this wedding feast, though not complete, will continue into eternity, melting away the boundaries that we often feel so keenly between heaven and earth, time and eternity, our longings and the fulfillment and completion that surely will come.

The prophet Isaiah's vision that God will swallow up death, wipe away the tears from all faces, and remove the disgrace of his people, and instead provide a feast of rich food and well-aged wine has begun in the life and ministry of Jesus Christ (Isa. 25:6–8). The Hebrew prophets instilled in God's people a longing for a future redemption, when the harmonious times of Eden, the garden of delight, will be restored. Wine will flow in great abundance.

When Christ transformed water into a great abundance of wine at the wedding feast of Cana, he provided a powerful sign that in him these promises of old have come to be fulfilled. Rather than seeing the miracle of Cana as mere symbol or picturesque illustration hinting at greater spiritual realties, however, we can—and must—see in it the manifestation of God's presence with his people and his desire to redeem all of creation. The gift of wine will always remain a visible expression of God's blessing and his desire to rejoice with his people and make them glad.

It should not be surprising, then, that Jesus spent so much time eating and drinking with people, many of them outsiders and on the fringe of society, lacking respectability. It was a mark of his ministry to share their joys and their sorrows as he dipped his bread in olive oil and sipped wine from the cup offered to him as a sign of hospitality. That did not always sit well with the religious establishment. No wonder they accused him of being a glutton and drunkard (Matt. 11:19; Luke 7:34).

PART 2

WHAT WOULD THE SAINTS DRINK?

Wine in the History of the Church

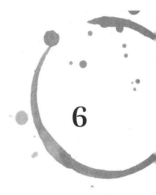

6

When the Saints
Sipped Wine

*Wine was given to make us cheerful, not to make us
behave shamefully; to make us laugh, not a laughing-
stock; to make us healthy, not sick; to mend the
weakness of the body, not to undermine the soul.*
—Saint John Chrysostom[1]

What Christ had instituted in his practice to share meals and enjoy wine with those whose lives he wanted to touch, the early church continued with great conviction. They celebrated a regular *agape* feast (*agape* from the Greek meaning "love") with food and wine, and it seems that at least for the first two centuries during this agape meal believers also celebrated the Lord's Supper. Believers came together to share a meal, remember Christ's death with bread and wine, and celebrate their new and communal life in Christ (1 Cor. 11:17–34; 12:12–31; Acts 2:46).

Once individuals from many different cultural, ethnic, and socioeconomic backgrounds, Christians were now one community:

the body of Christ. This unity was central to their new identity in Christ. And the highest form of this spiritual life was the love that they had for each other despite all their obvious differences. The agape meal was meant to be an expression of this loving union, and yet the early church, just like us today, struggled to keep this unity. (1 Cor. 1:17–22, 13; Jude 1:12, 20–21).

For the early church, the Christian life wasn't an individual journey. Christians were baptized into a new form of life. They were now members of a new family held together by God's Holy Spirit (1 Cor. 12:12–13).[2] They practiced no personal quiet time or individual Bible study, though the apostle Paul did encourage them to pray without ceasing with the help of the Holy Spirit (1 Thess. 5:17; Eph. 6:18; Rom. 12:12).

Their spiritual life was foremost a communal affair, expressed most profoundly as they gathered for this shared love feast and the celebration of the Lord's Supper (1 Cor. 11:17–34). As they ate from the one bread and drank wine from the one cup and lingered over a shared meal, it instilled in them that this newfound life was a gift of union with Christ *and* each other. In this new community they were called to subvert traditional hierarchical structures. Just as Christ lowered himself to become a servant and poor, so were they to learn to hold in highest regard those whom they normally wouldn't give the time of the day, those whom society often looked down on. The seemingly weak have great standing in Jesus' kingdom. They are indispensable. As the body of Christ, they learned to share each other's sorrows and celebrate each other's successes no matter their standing in society (1 Cor. 12:20–26; Phil. 2:4–8).

This unity was a remarkable act of faith, because Christ had brought together a rather diverse and seemingly incompatible bunch of people: reverent Jews and pagans with strange spiritual practices in their background, rich and poor, slaves and free, some respected and well established in society and some outcasts who did not really fit anywhere. What better place to practice this than around the same table, sharing the same food, and drinking the same wine?

As you might imagine, this spiritual truth of being made one in Christ gave rise to many challenges as they practiced it on the ground. Perhaps it is not surprising that in the class-conscious society of Corinth, a Roman colony where the church was especially diverse, Christians found it difficult to practice unity. Apparently, some well-to-do Christians began eating and drinking separately and had lavish private meals. While they indulged in food and wine—some even got intoxicated from drinking too much wine—others left the agape feast hungry.[3]

Paul was infuriated by these practices that had torn the church in Corinth apart. To him, they undermined the work of Christ and the church's new identity as the body of Christ (1 Cor. 10:17; 11:17–34). Paul's instructions for celebrating the Lord's Supper, which we most often hear so serenely in our liturgy quite apart from this distressing context, follow immediately after his words of outrage and reveal how crucial it was to him that believers keep the agape feast properly: as the great equalizer in God's presence.

I still marvel that it was a meal that glued the early Christians together and that it was the bread they chewed and the wine they savored that helped them ingest this radical new identity they shared in Christ. And for Paul, it is the Holy Spirit that unites believers both in their baptism and as they drink from the eucharistic cup: "we were all made to drink of one Spirit" (1 Cor. 12:13).

This newfound identity and unity weren't meant to be a lofty spiritual idea floating about in the sky but a hands-on reality that worked itself out most profoundly in their shared meals. Who was eating with whom, what kind of food they ate, and what kind of wine they drank mattered. They were all markers of status and could either unite or divide, transgress class boundaries or fortify them.

That is not so different from our times today. Whom we choose to have over for dinner and what kind of food and wine we serve are indicators of our values and whom we value. We all want to find our "tribe," but both Christ and Paul challenge us to rethink tribal tendencies in light of our identity as the body of Christ. Our circle of friends and family must expand to include God's family.

Who we open our doors to and welcome at our tables and share meals with reveals much about what we believe the meaning of the

Christian life to be. Even if we are on a tight budget, we still choose where our extra money goes. Are our habits in line with Jesus' teaching that we receive all, and especially outsiders, as if they were Christ himself? It would be a good spiritual practice to prayerfully think about this and see where God might lead you.

The life of the early church was challenging because Christians often experienced persecution. However, this did not deter them from gathering for the agape feast and the Lord's Supper, eating and drinking in each other's homes with real food and real wine, not thin wafers and a tiny sip of wine or grape juice as we do today. It was a much more sensuous affair, bringing some comfort and joy into lives marred by persecution and profound suffering.

Wine remained a staple and Christians enjoyed wine in their religious celebrations, family feasts, and everyday life whenever possible. Paul's advice to Timothy gives witness to this: "No longer drink only water, but take a little wine for the sake of your stomach and your frequent ailments" (1 Tim. 5:23).[4] The story of the Good Samaritan also hints at the rich medicinal practices of Roman times and how wine was applied to disinfect wounds (Luke 10:34). You might be surprised to learn that wine remained the major medicine in Europe and North America until the nineteenth century. Wine was also an important commodity for trade (Rev. 18:13). Because it was a staple, people were worried that its cost might increase (Rev. 6:6). Wine remained a consistent part of the lives of early Christians, just as it had for Jesus and his followers.

However, as early as the second century, dissenting voices emerged. Various heretical groups, like the Encratites, Hydroparastatae, and Severians, spread teaching that it really was women and wine rather than the passions of the heart that were leading some Christians astray. It will always remain a great temptation to focus outward and lay blame elsewhere for the battles and temptations we experience, whether they come from within or from societal pressures.[5]

These heretics belonged to Gnostic groups that emphasized the spiritual over the material. Within their dualist worldview, they believed that matter was inherently flawed and taught abstention from wine and sex as marks of a truly spiritual life. The Hydroparastatae even refused to use wine in the Eucharist and used water instead.

Saint Cyprian (AD 200–259), the bishop of Carthage in Africa, was the first theologian to write a defense of wine. He was a wise leader, knew Scripture well, and wasn't going to stray from Jesus' teachings. He wrote, "In offering the cup, the teachings of the Lord must be observed and we must do exactly as the Lord first did Himself for us—the cup which is offered up in remembrance of Him is to be offered mixed with wine."[6] He boldly praised wine as a gift and blessing from God and went so far as to say that the absence of wine was a lack of spiritual grace.[7] Cyprian also insisted that the offering the church brings to the Lord's Supper had to correspond to the suffering of Christ. The crushing of the grapes and the fermentation of grape juice into wine capture Christ's suffering, death, and resurrection beautifully and reminded the believer that their suffering too would lead into the life of the resurrection. For Cyprian the form (wine) needed to conform to the content (the suffering of Christ) in order to reveal the meaning of the cross. Cyprian also astutely recognized that in the Bible, wine is a key theme and symbol for the eschatological age (the age to come). As an act of obedience to the teachings of Christ, the early church continued to use wine in the celebration of the Lord's Supper.[8]

Many church fathers, such as Saint Irenaeus, Saint Clement of Alexandria, Saint John Chrysostom, and Saint Augustine followed suit and praised wine as a gift from God and affirmed its goodness, understanding it as a mediator between heaven and earth.[9]

As persecution eased and Roman Emperor Constantine legalized Christianity, slowly but surely a new trend occurred: no longer suffering the threat of persecution and being outsiders, some Christians became lax, lost the edge to their radical faith, and settled into a more comfortable and even indulgent lifestyle.

Saint Chrysostom's wise words about wine might give us a glimpse into the new tensions Christians found themselves in: "Wine was given to make us cheerful, not to make us behave shamefully; to make us laugh, not a laughing-stock; to make us healthy, not sick; to mend the weakness of the body, not to undermine the soul."[10] It became increasingly difficult to juggle the call to follow Christ and live amid the lures of the Roman Empire.

Not all were able or willing to live in these tensions. Instead, some Christians, feeling the pull toward a more radical Christian life, fled into the deserts of Egypt and Syria and later Palestine. What Saint Anthony had modeled at the close of the third century, thousands of others sought to imitate in the fourth and fifth centuries. We now call them the desert fathers and mothers. At first it was just a few radicals like Saint Anthony, but over time it became a trend to leave the "world" behind and find healing and spiritual wholeness in the extremes of desert isolation. The barren and fierce landscape of the desert provided fertile ground for inner purgation but wasn't a place to grow vines or learn how to enjoy God's gifts in a wholesome and holy way.[11]

To this day, the insights of the desert fathers and mothers inspire and offer pathways to soul care and healing. However, their extreme ascetical practices married with their desire to kill the passions of the body remain hugely problematic. Some of the desert fathers revived the heresy that women and wine were sources of great temptation and that the only way to deal with them was to flee more deeply into the desert.

Feasts and celebrations weren't part of their spirituality, but once in a while they did drink wine when it was served in the Eucharist. It was a no-nonsense kind of spirituality. In its spiritual prowess, it laid the foundation for a new monastic movement that emerged farther west in Gaul (today Europe), albeit with some major adjustments, especially when it came to the drinking and enjoyment of wine.

While the desert fathers and mothers sought purity of heart and to win their neighbors over to Christ with a radical pursuit of humility and self-denial, some Christians in the western part of the Roman Empire (Gaul), especially in what is now Italy and France, also sought a more reclusive life, yet without the radical denial of earthly pleasures such as wine. Both Italy and France had a long history in viticulture and wine drinking reaching back many centuries. The Romans only intensified it and made sure that there was always plentiful wine for their soldiers and citizens.

Saint Martin of Tours (316–97) is perhaps one of the most important early Christian saints who took a radical turn away from the prestigious life of a Roman soldier to become a humble servant of Christ and seek out a monastic lifestyle. He grew up in what we would call an upper-middle-class pagan family, with his father holding a senior position in the Roman army. When he was young, his family settled in the fertile wine region of what is now Pavia along the Ticino River in northern Italy. They enjoyed all the benefits of Roman citizens: a nice estate, servants, a good education, and lots of good food and delicious wines. The Romans planted vineyards wherever they could, so Martin's childhood home might very well have been surrounded by vineyards, and he might have grown up learning about growing, grafting, and cultivating vines and how to make wine. Martin, following in his father's footsteps, became a soldier for the Roman Empire.

When Martin made the radical decision to part with his pagan past and break his vow to serve the emperor as a Roman soldier, he left behind all the privileges and rights of a Roman citizen. A poor man and estranged from his family, Martin moved to France to study theology with Hilary of Poitiers, whose theology was markedly different from that of the desert fathers. Eventually Martin settled near Tours in the fertile Loire region of France to live as a hermit and spread the gospel.

Tours is happily situated on the fertile banks of the Loire River, and to this day this area is known for its great wines. Perhaps his childhood experience of growing up in the lush region of Pavia along the Ticino River in Italy inspired him to settle in yet another wine region where the Loire River shapes the landscape into fertile terroir for growing vines and crafting wines of excellence.

Legend has it that Martin not only spurred on the development of viticulture in his new home but also tried his hand in viticulture himself. It is said that he discovered wild Chenin vines in the nearby Touraine forests and grafted them into what we know today as a Chenin Noir. Among the many miracles attributed to him are the replenishment of empty wine jars, following in the tradition of his beloved Jesus.[12] Saint Martin is the patron saint of new wine in Slovenia, and he is celebrated each year on November 11, when the grape juice has just gone through the fermentation process and become new wine. In the Catholic Church, Saint Martin is the patron saint of vintners and wine growers.

Have you ever wondered why we remember Saint Martin's generosity to the poor and his profound humility but rarely hear that he took an interest in viticulture and wine? That is quite telling about what teachers prioritize when they recount the stories of our Christian saints.

Martin became a great evangelist traveling all over Gaul, and his legacy endures to this day, especially in France, where more than 3500 churches are dedicated to him. The great reformer Martin Luther is named after Saint Martin, and Saint Martin's Day is still celebrated in many parts of Europe with a delicious feast of roasted goose and well-crafted wine, preferably from the Loire region. Saint Martin and the rich history of wine in the Loire Valley can inspire us as we ponder how to embrace wine as a gift from God, rather than avoid it by fleeing into the desert.

When the Saints
Planted Vineyards

Of the Quantity of drink: . . . we think one hemina
of wine a day is sufficient for each one.
—Saint Benedict, *The Rule of St. Benedict*

It is to Christian nuns and monks that we owe the amazingly rich history of viticulture and wine in Europe and beyond. No monk has shaped Western Christianity and viticulture more than Saint Benedict of Nursia in Italy (ca. AD 480–547). He was born amid much political and social turmoil, and the times were radically different from those of Saint Martin of Tours. The Roman Empire had gradually declined and finally collapsed with the fall of Rome.

As the political, economic, and social structures of the Roman Empire broke away, slowly but surely new monastic communities emerged. Visionary monks were trying to figure out how to live together during these trying and chaotic times. Saint Benedict wrote his *Rule* to regulate the daily life of the monks, a rule that brought stability, rhythm, and vision in a time that lacked it all. It became the most popular rule to organize monastic communities during the Middle Ages.

The *Rule* regulates the lives of the monks into a rhythm of prayer, study, and manual labor and draws profoundly on the Bible as it envisions their life together. Hospitality was central to their vocation to embody the life and teaching of Christ in their midst.

Benedict wrote, "Let all guests who arrive be received like Christ, for He is going to say, 'I came as a guest, and you received Me' (Matt. 25:35). And to all let due honor be shown, especially to the domestics of the faith and to pilgrims."[1]

In this ministry of hospitality, Saint Benedict gave special attention to the cellar master, who oversaw the distribution of food and wine. He had to be of superior spiritual maturity and a wise man, with an even temper, frugal and honest. Benedict instructed the cellar master to provide amply for the guests, the poor, and the sick. For Benedict, all the food and the wine they served were like sacred vessels of the altar, revealing something about God's benevolence and generosity.[2] Therefore the work of the cellar master was just as important as that of the priests who administered the Eucharist.

Saint Benedict had a profound vision of the sacredness of the material world, including the agricultural work the monks performed and the food and wine they made. All work was a spiritual vocation whether a monk worked in the wine cellar or out in the vineyards pruning vines or in the kitchen baking bread. These were not secular matters, disconnected from their spiritual lives, but matters imbued with spiritual meaning because Benedict understood them to be part of God's good creation.

The *Rule* pays a surprising amount of time discussing the nitty-gritty details of daily life, including what monks were to eat, drink, and wear. Just as we do today, Benedict understood that one's appearance, what one wears, what one eats and drinks, and with whom one shares meals are expressions of one's status in society and helps define and cement hierarchical structures within society. Saint Benedict was keenly aware of this and wanted to make sure that within the walls of the monastery, all were the same before God. And this foundational belief had to be expressed in how they lived together as a community. For this reason, Benedict prescribed that all monks had to wear the same clothes, eat the same food, and receive the same amount of wine—yes, monks received a daily allotment of wine.

Saint Benedict was hesitant to allow his monks to drink wine. He was quite taken with the radical teachings of the desert fathers who rejected wine in fear it would lead them astray. He studied their teachings closely, and all Benedictine monks had to read John Cassian, who had collected the wisdom of the desert fathers and brought their teachings to Europe. Torn in his desire to follow the radical teaching of the desert fathers but surrounded by a vibrant wine culture, Benedict realized that it was unrealistic to forbid his monks to drink wine. Italians had a long history of vine growing and wine drinking going back at least to the Etruscans in 900 BC. Many of the great wines of the Roman Empire had once come from Italy, and wine drinking was deeply embedded in Italian culture. And of course the Bible was full of references to wine as a gift from God, and Jesus celebrated the Lord's Supper with wine. Hesitatingly, Saint Benedict recognized the importance of adjusting his teachings to his cultural context. He writes, "It is with some hesitation . . . that we determine the measure of nourishment for others. However, making allowance for the weakness of the infirm, we think one hemina of wine a day is sufficient for each one. . . . If the circumstance of the place, or the work, or the summer's heat should require more, let that depend on the judgment of the Superior, who must above all things see to it that excess or drunkenness do not creep in."[3]

One can see the wisdom and pastoral care Saint Benedict exerts in his advice. He is cautious, but also generous. Though he gives an exact measure of one hemina of wine per day for each monk, he realizes that particular circumstances might call for greater amounts of wine. He trusts that the abbot or the cellar master will be able to administer the portions wisely and warns of the danger of excess and drunkenness. Given that monks were called to a more ascetical lifestyle, this allotment might seem generous to us. However, the surrounding culture most likely drank a lot more wine per day than just one hemina.

In addition to the daily allowance of wine, the monks needed wine for the celebration of the Eucharist, for tending to the sick and poor, and of course for their extensive ministry of hospitality. No wonder that the monks and nuns took to planting vineyards and crafting wine.

How much wine was one hemina? It is a Roman measurement, and we don't quite know whether Benedict's hemina would have equaled a Roman hemina. However, there is agreement that it would have been about a third of a liter, more than a third of a bottle of wine or more than half a pint in contemporary measurements. In a restaurant today that adds up to about two or three glasses of wine, depending on the size of the pour. According to medical studies, this amount of wine stays within the realm of what is considered healthy for the body.

This small paragraph on wine in the *Rule of St. Benedict* changed the fate of wine and Christianity in Europe for good. Little did Benedict know how inspiring this allowance of wine would be in shaping the wine world of Europe to this day. As the monks and nuns spread throughout Europe to start new monastic settlements, they also planted vineyards and crafted wine as part of their mission. Some of the most famous vineyards in countries like Italy, Germany, and France hearken back to these Benedictine monks and nuns following the *Rule of St. Benedict.*

One of the remarkable features of the Benedictine movement was its vision for an integrated lifestyle of daily worship, study, and manual labor. Every monk had to be involved in all three vocations. No one was excused from manual labor. Cultivating the land and producing one's own food and wine were just as much part of their mission as living a life of worship and studying Scripture. As they sang through the Psalter weekly, at least once a week they would have sung Psalm 104, a psalm that praises God as the creator and provider and singles out wine as a gift from God to gladden human hearts. The psalm instilled in them the belief that this earth is God's good creation and wine a precious gift to bring them joy and gladness.

Just as the Israelites understood God's promises and blessings to be fulfilled as they settled into a land of plenty, so did the monks and nuns see their new mission field in Europe as a promised land that they were to settle and cultivate. Had not the patriarchs and prophets of old spoken of God's blessing in terms of a fruitful land with an abundance of grain, olive oil, and wine? Would God not restore paradise so they could live in peace and safety at a time when the world seemed to be falling apart? Surely these monks and nuns believed that the planting of vines and crafting of wine were tangible signs of God's blessing and benevolence.

These monks and nuns had a profound belief that God wanted to restore paradise here on earth and that they would play an important role in bringing this to pass. God's kingdom was surely an agricultural one, and the plentiful fruit that they harvested each year reminded them of God's abundant generosity.

As the infrastructure of the Roman Empire fell apart and as social structures gave way to unstable and at times chaotic social conditions, the monasteries and convents emerged as peaceful centers of faith, learning, and agriculture with beautiful gardens gracing monastic settlements. Did not God create order out of chaos? Could not the monasteries and convents become those places where chaos had to give way to order, rhythm, and peace so that life as God intended it could flourish? Were not the monastic gardens glimpses into paradise restored here on earth?

The Benedictine movement remained relatively small until some monks settled into the fertile hills of Cluny in Burgundy, France, around AD 910. From there they sent out groups of monks to bring the gospel to other parts of Gaul. By AD 1100 the abbot of Cluny oversaw between 1,300 and 1,500 monasteries that had been started all over Europe, each setting up a place of worship and planting fields, vineyards, and fruit trees, seeing paradise restored as they sang the Psalms and prayed a new epoch of Christian history into being. By faith they planted orchards and vineyards, crafting beautiful wine for the celebration of the Eucharist and the feasts of the Christian year, bringing heaven down to earth.

Worship became increasingly elaborate, and Cluny Abbey became a popular pilgrimage site, drawing pilgrims from all over the Holy Roman Empire. A new political structure emerged with Cluny Abbey deeply involved as a spiritual and political center. And as Cluny Abbey received more donations of land and eager pilgrims supported its mission, the monks became successful entrepreneurs. A vision for a magnificent abbey became reality when they started building what became one of the wonders of the world: Cluny Abbey. They began building it in 1088 and it was completed in 1130. Notre Dame in Paris was modeled after it but lacked the great splendor of Cluny. It was an unbelievably majestic and glorious sight and continued to draw pilgrims and tourists throughout the Middle Ages. Surely the wine for the Eucharist had to match the splendor and grandeur of this magnificent abbey, and monks went about perfecting the wines of Burgundy, where Cluny was located.

Cluny Abbey was destroyed during the French Revolution and now lies in ruins. Some of the pillars of the abbey were preserved and are housed in museums in Cluny and Paris. I went to visit these museums many years ago and was struck by these pillars, which depict scenes of the garden of Eden and paradise restored. Grape vines and grape leaves adorn these pillars that once upheld one of the most magnificent abbeys of Western Christendom. What astonished me was that the architecture of their place of worship reminded the monks and nuns every day that the foundation of the church was God's good creation. The vines hewn into stone pillars reaching up into the sky baptized their imagination to see that wine is indeed a gift of creation meant to inspire heavenly communion.

To match the splendor of the abbey in Cluny, the monks also needed beautifully crafted wine that was suitable to be used in such a majestic place of worship. In their desire to glorify God in all things, they went on a mission to craft wine that would honor God with its beauty and delicacy like a sweet fragrance wafting up into God's presence. Over years, decades, and even centuries, the Benedictines sought to perfect their craft as vintners.

Monks were sent to the now famous Côte d'Or in Burgundy, a fertile valley, to plant vine-

Capital featuring Adam and Eve at the Basilica of Sainte-Marie-Madeleine in Vezelay. *Public domain.*

yards and craft wines for the flourishing monastic center of Cluny. About sixty miles north of Cluny, they built Abbaye Saint-Vivant to house the monks whose life work was to plant vineyards in the surrounding hills and craft wine of exceptional quality. Wayside shrines and crosses along the vineyards reminded them to stop for prayer, and all their work was saturated with a profound sense of God's presence in their midst.[4] Over time these dedicated monks developed a careful understanding of the land and what parcels were most suitable for planting vineyards. They discerned the terroir of particular parcels of land with their infinite and intricate complexities. These vineyards are today recognized as the Grand Crus of Burgundy, producing some of the most ethereal and beautiful wines the world has ever tasted.

The ruins of Abbaye Saint-Vivant nestled in the hills of Vergy still remind us of the great legacy that these monks left behind. Inspired by Isaac's visionary blessing of the dew of heaven and the fatness of the earth, and plenty of grain and wine (Gen. 27:28) and Saint Benedict's *Rule*, they planted vineyards and harvested plenty of grapes—all as tangible signs of God's blessing upon them. The garden of Eden seemed restored in the golden valley of Burgundy's Côte d'Or and in many other parts of Europe—at least for a time.

Every year, I lead a wine pilgrimage to Burgundy and take our pilgrims to this special place, where we touch history and walk the vineyards that these monks planted so long ago. It is an incredibly moving experience to touch those ancient walls, walk through the wine cellars below, and envision monks singing the Psalms as they tended to the vines and crafted wines to the glory of God. The ruins of Abbaye Saint-Vivant are being lovingly restored, and our annual wine pilgrimage has coincided with the slow restoration of a place once forgotten. Perhaps one day it will become a vibrant pilgrimage site. For now, we are lonesome pilgrims savoring this tucked-away treasure of Christian history and agrarian spirituality.

By the eleventh century, Benedictine monasteries owned all of the now-famous Grand Cru vineyards of Burgundy stretching from Macon to Beaune to Dijon, with now world-famous wine villages such as Puligny-Montrachet, Meursault, Volnay, Pommard, Vosne-Romanée, and Gevrey-Chambertin in between. Little reminds us today in the cultural landscape of Burgundy of the rich Christian heritage of these vineyards. A single and solitary stone cross in front of the most famous vineyard in Burgundy and really in the whole world, Romanée-Conti, still reminds us that it was Christian monks who first planted these vineyards. When you drink a glass of well-crafted Chardonnay, Pinot Noir, or Riesling, remember that we owe these stunning cultural treasures to these pioneering monks and nuns whose life work was to glorify God in all things, including a glass of well-crafted wine.

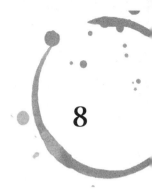

8

Tipsy Monks and the Fragrance of the Reformation

If I do not eat his flesh and do not drink his blood, I will
not have his life in me. . . . To hold him and to embrace
him is a joyous feast, to consume him is eternal life.
—Bernard of Clairvaux[1]

The Benedictines Come of Age

As the monks and nuns established monasteries and convents all over Europe and what is now the United Kingdom, vineyard planting and wine drinking became more common not only in southern and central Europe but even in places like northern Germany, Denmark, and England, where beer drinking had been the norm.[2] French monasteries provided wine to areas where wine growing wasn't possible. In 610 Saint Columbanus at Nantes, France, shipped wines to his Celtic brothers in Ireland. By the time of Bede (AD 690–735), even the Irish monks and nuns had planted vineyards. You can see a wine strainer that the Celtic monks would have used displayed in the National Museum of Ireland.[3]

Perhaps it is still hard for us to envision how important wine was to these monastic communities. From the early church well into the Middle Ages, everyone—priests, monks, nuns, and laypeople alike—received both bread and wine in the celebration of the Eucharist. During the Middle Ages many peasants came to the monastery to join the service, and wine was often offered afterward to continue the celebration. Monks and nuns celebrated the Eucharist daily, and wine was served during the many feast days that were celebrated in the Middle Ages. It was only in the fourteenth century that wine began to be withheld from laypeople in the Catholic Church, and this issue of whether the laity should receive wine turned into a major battleground during the Reformation.[4] Needless to say, vineyards and wine featured prominently in the monastic communities, and traces of it can still be seen in many places, especially in Europe.

Saint Benedict had emphasized the importance of hospitality, and every monastery had a guesthouse where travelers and pilgrims were able to find rest and nourishment for a few days. He wrote, "Let all guests who arrive be received as Christ, because He is going to say: 'I came as a guest, and you received Me.'"[5] The guests received free food and wine. We have to remember that in those days, ordinary people's diet was very simple and often lacked nutrients, so wine became an important source not only of fluids but also nutrients such as vitamins and minerals.

The care of the sick was also an integral part of Saint Benedict's monastic vision: "Before and above all things, care must be taken of the sick, so they be served as if they were Christ in person; for He Himself said, 'I was sick, and you visited Me.'"[6] Each monastery had to establish a small hospital room, and with it they cultivated an herb garden to provide medicine for the sick. Wine was used as medicine in a wide range of applications. Herbal tinctures were made with wine, and wine was prescribed as a nutrient, an internal antiseptic, and a restorative.

It was Benedictines who founded the medical school of Salerno in the tenth century. The *Salernitan Rule of Health* prescribed wine more frequently than any other therapeutic agent.[7] The poor and the sick, the orphans and the elderly found refuge in these charitable hospitals, and having a steady supply of wine was crucial.

When the Roman Empire had crumbled and the monasteries emerged as centers of faith, learning, and charity, it truly seemed that God's kingdom had come in the form of these communities. Continual worship was offered up to God, the monks' and nuns' lives were saturated with prayer, and they lived together in peace. They plowed their fields and pruned their vines. They enjoyed the fruit of the earth and shared it with the poor. The sick were healed, the orphans found a home, and the elderly were comforted and cared for. Heaven did come to earth in these agriculturally grounded Christian communities, at least for a time.

The Decline of Benedictine Spirituality at Cluny

This idyllic life, if ever it was, did not last. Cluny in particular became increasingly famous as a spiritual and educational center. A reform of the worship style at Cluny made it difficult to hold on to the threefold way of life with equal time given to worship, study, and manual labor. Singing the liturgy now became the monks' most important occupation. Saint Benedict ordered that the 150 psalms were to be sung once a week. At their most extreme, the monks of Cluny sang 210 psalms a day, and there was no time left for the lowly work of manual labor. Slowly but surely monks excused themselves from manual labor and devoted their lives to prayer and study only.

Eventually Cluny also became a powerful economic and political center. Saint Benedict had imagined and set forth in his *Rule* that each monastery should function independently. However, an abbot of Cluny, to ensure uniformity of rite within the Benedictine movement, was able to reform the system in such a way that he would oversee all the other Benedictine monasteries and exert direct and unlimited power over them. In the latter part of the eleventh century, abbot Hugh of Cluny controlled more than 1,300 monasteries, and the wealth that the abbey amassed because of its influence and connections was directly poured into building the most magnificent Romanesque abbey of Christendom, Cluny Abbey.

As is so often the case, once these Benedictine monks of Cluny became successful, wealthy, and significant power brokers in the political arena of a profoundly feudal society, their spirituality suffered. Going through the motions of incessant liturgical prac-tices, surrounded by the lavish splendor of Cluny Abbey and over-indulging in food and wine, they had forgotten Saint Benedict's vision. By the end of the eleventh century, the monks of Cluny had lost their spiritual prowess, and voices of discontent emerged. Even as the monks' spiritual vitality was fading, the majestic abbey beck-oned throngs of pilgrims into their fold.

Cluny Abbey was completed in 1130. It had five aisles with high barrel-vaulted naves and beautiful chapels attached at the east end. The abbey was surmounted by octagonal towers and was composed of a three-story elevation consisting of slim aisles with pointed arches. It was a majestic sight and drew many pilgrims. The liturgy became ever more lavish and elaborate, the vestments were made of the finest fabric, stonework was clad in gold, and the sound of the choir was angelic. Cluny library became the richest and finest library in all of Europe. Most pilgrims who came to this majestic place of worship would have stood in awe at such an expression of splendor and majesty, wealth, and power.

By now the monks of Cluny had long given up manual labor and saw the fields and vineyards surrounding the monastery only from the distance of their cloistered lives. Abbots became managers and brokers, mediators and advisors to kings and popes. A hierarchy of power and influence emerged within a new feudal society, and the abbots and some of the monks of Cluny stood at the top of the hierarchy. Their lives became more indulgent, sourcing goods and wine from other monasteries to ensure that the receptions at Cluny would match the splendor of its sumptuous abbey and international reputation. A thirteenth-century manuscript illustration of an abbey cellar master secretly sipping wine in the wine cellar of the abbey hints at the indulgence that became an increasing problem in the successful monasteries of the Benedictines.

The glorious glamour, together with the feudal politics that Cluny Abbey had helped establish, directly undermined the spirit of the *Rule of St. Benedict*, where simplicity, equality of all before God, and manual labor

An abbey cellarer testing his wine. Illumination from a copy of Li livres dou santé by Aldobrandino of Siena. British Library, Sloane 2435, f. 44v. Public domain.

were fundamental to the monastic life. The fame, economic success, and political power of Cluny did not bode well for the spiritual health of this monastic community and slowly eroded its spiritual life from within. The splendid worship style and comfortable life of the monks stood in stark contrast not only to the poverty of the peasant population surrounding the monastery but also to the vision of their founding father, Saint Benedict. Bernard of Clairvaux, a reformer of whom we will learn shortly, wrote scourging words in judgment of Cluny: "Oh vanity of vanities, yet no more vain than insane! The church is resplendent in her walls and wanting in her poor. She dressed her stones in gold and lets her sons go naked."[8] A cry for reform arose not far from the boisterous Cluny Abbey.

A Cry for Reform: The Cistercians

A two-day walk from Cluny Abbey in the fertile valley of the Côte d'Or near the small village of Citeaux, monks gathered and committed their lives once more to the true spirit of the *Rule of St. Benedict*. To this day, the Cistercians are named after this small village of Citeaux. Disillusioned with Cluny, these monks sought to live out the ideals of the *Rule* with renewed vigor.[9] A return to manual labor and severe ascetical practices was one of the hallmarks of the Cistercian reform movement. Cistercians became impassioned farmers, excelling at managing forests, planting vineyards, and crafting wines of great beauty. The artwork of their illuminated manuscripts gives witness to this renewed agricultural vigor and a glimpse into their ability to create artifacts of great beauty.

The monks chose well when they settled near Citeaux by Dijon, along the now famous valley of the Côte d'Or, as it provided ample opportunity to develop agriculture. As they returned to the threefold life of worship, study, and manual labor, their saintly reputation spread quickly, and local nobility supported their new endeavors. Inspired once more by the Bible and the *Rule of St. Benedict*, they made it a priority to plant vineyards, so they had wine for the celebration of the Eucharist and their daily needs, for their ministry of hospitality, and for tending to the sick. They drained swamps, cleared woodlands, and built waterways for the irrigation of their fields and vineyards.

It was the Cistercians in Burgundy who first developed the concept of the "cru," which is so important for evaluating the quality of wine in France even to this day.[10] They learned to identify the best plots of land for cultivating vines and were able to hone their skills as vintners. The Cistercians first planted the vineyard of Clos de Vougeot. This now famous vineyard did not come into existence all at once. Over time the monks shrewdly added parcel to parcel of land, planted vines, and surrounded this vast vineyard with a stone wall, which created a unique microclimate. The monks also began selecting and planting vines from the Pinot Noir variety that would grow only small clusters and bring a low yield with much higher quality. To increase the quality even more, they also started blending the best wines from various parts of this vast vineyard. It is a highlight for me when I get to take my wine pilgrims to this vineyard and allow them to walk into it, observe the vines, meditate there, and sense the rich Christian history in vine growing and wine crafting. It is an impressive sight beckoning wine lovers from all over the world.

Given that the Cistercians' highest vocation was to worship God and glorify him in all things, perhaps it should not surprise us that crafting wine became part of their pursuit for spiritual perfection. The wines that they were able to craft from Clos de Vougeot became stunningly beautiful and renowned throughout the lands. Over time, the reputation of the wines from Clos de Vougeot vineyard surpassed any others in the Holy Roman Empire and lasted well into the nineteenth century. The Cistercians had no doubt that their pursuit of perfection should be applied to all spheres of life, including the crafting of the most beautiful wines that they could possibly craft. The famous wine writer Hugh Johnson argues that the Cistercians made Clos de Vougeot "the laboratory of their pursuit of perfection."[11] In the film *Babette's Feast*, at a climactic moment Babette serves wine from Clos de Vougeot, pouring forth the most delicious wine to reveal the spiritual power that both food and wine can impart to receptive guests.[12]

These same Cistercian monks also built the first industrial winery of the Middle Ages right beside the vineyard Clos de Vougeot. The winery is a museum today and houses some of the oldest winepresses of Europe. It is an impressive sight to see these massive winepresses and imagine monks working them during harvest season. They still give witness to the monks' incredible technological ingenuity in harnessing power to press the ever-increasing number of grapes they harvested. It is one of my favorite stops on our wine pilgrimages because it is so easy to imagine monks working these winepresses as they chanted the Psalms together. And the walled-in vineyard of Clos de Vougeot always makes me think of the garden of Eden, the garden of pleasure and delight, where Adam and Eve once lived in harmony with God and the earth and took pleasure and delight in all they ate and drank.

The Cistercian monks strove to glorify God in all they did. Planting vineyards and crafting wine was one way to honor their creator and redeemer God. We often forget that these monks received the Eucharist daily and would drink from the Eucharist cup before they went out into the vineyards and cellars to perfect their winecrafting skills. They weren't like us, distracted by social media, sports competitions, and trips to the shopping malls. Their lives were simple and focused in ways that most of us can't even imagine anymore. Sometimes I wonder whether the monks were competing with each other to make the most beautiful and ethereal wines to host the presence of Christ in their midst. An illuminated manuscript of the book of Job, created by the early Cistercians, shows a monk harvesting grapes from a grape vine.[13] It reveals how important their agricultural work was for them as an act of worship. As they tilled the soil, planted vines, and harvested grapes, they sang their psalms and meditated on Scripture. As they worked toward the perfection of their own lives, they sought to perfect all that they offered to God, including the wine they crafted for the most holy celebration of the Eucharist.

The Cistercians remained a small reform movement until a charismatic leader named Saint Bernard of Clairvaux drew many young men away from their families to join this impassioned man of God. His charismatic zeal ensured that the Cistercians grew into a considerable movement. By the time of Bernard's death in 1153, the Cistercians had founded 343 monasteries all over Europe. By the middle of the thirteenth century, they had founded 647 monasteries and as many nunneries. They searched out the lonely places throughout Europe, established communities of worship there, and went to work in the fields and forests, planting vineyards and gardens, bringing heaven down to earth as they celebrated the Eucharist with wine from their newly planted vineyards. Christianity spread throughout Europe, and so did the cultivation of vineyards and the crafting of wine. Wine, together with beer and mead, became the primary source of safe fluids during the Middle Ages in Europe, especially where the monks and nuns were able to cultivate vineyards. Water remained an unstable source of liquids because it often carried and spread diseases.

It is an intriguing fact that the Cistercians became fascinated with the Song of Songs, the one book in the Bible that celebrated both wine and sex as gifts from God. It is the most sensual book of the Bible. Bernard of Clairvaux wrote eighty-six sermons on it. Jewish and Christian theologians had written about it for centuries, but Bernard took it to new heights of mystical reflection on the union between Christ and the believer.

Bernard had grown up along the Côte d'Or in Clairvaux, Burgundy, and must have been inspired by the vineyards and wine of his youth to dedicate much of his time to interpreting the Song of Songs, this great love poem of the Bible. This sensuous book celebrates human sexuality as a gift from God, and the rich garden imagery hearkens back to the garden of Eden. Erotic love is compared to entering a lush garden and enjoying its fruit, including delicious wine: "Let him kiss me with the kisses of his mouth! For your love is better than wine" (Song 1:2). Bernard interprets the Songs of Songs allegorically and understands it to speak of God's great love affair, with Christ as the bridegroom and the believer or the church as his beloved.

Though Bernard's theology was extremely ascetical, it was profoundly impassioned by the idea that our relationship with God is that of a great love affair. He boldly embraced the sensual and sexual imagery of the Song of Songs to explore this loving relationship between Christ and the believer. The danger and tension that he saw was that believers get stuck in the materiality and sensuality of things as the monks of Cluny had done. For Bernard the sensuous realm of our existence is a gift that is to draw us nearer to our bridegroom, Jesus Christ. Perhaps there is no more intimate way to receive Christ than in bread and wine, and Bernard wrote in one of his letters, "If I do not eat his flesh and do not drink his blood, I will not have his life in me. . . . To hold him and to embrace him is a joyous feast, to consume him is eternal life."[14]

The Cistercians Need Reform

The Cistercians also became incredibly successful in their work, and over time they suffered a fate similar to that of the Benedictines. They became economically successful, politically influential, and spiritually lax. Reform movements continued to correct the path toward a more wholehearted devotion to Jesus Christ, the way of the cross, and the threefold life of prayer, study, and manual labor.

Other reform movements emerged, such as the Franciscans in Italy. Saint Francis of Assisi (1181–1226), the founder of the order, insisted that his order should not own any land and should remain devoted to a life of poverty, knowing how easily money and wealth could erode the life of faith. Even before his death, his brothers deviated from his wisdom and bought land. Over time this order too needed to be reformed.

In the fourteenth century, under the umbrella of the Dominican order, a new reform movement emerged called the Friends of God, made up of clergy and laypeople. They lived during one of the most troubled periods of medieval Europe, experiencing the Black Death, economic turmoil, incessant warfare, and papal schism that brought much instability to the church and the population at large. What was unique to this movement was their emphasis on lay communities committing themselves to a life set apart for Christ. One of their centers was located in Strasbourg, nestled along the Rhine River, with vineyards adorning its hills just like the Côte d'Or in Burgundy.

Johannes Tauler (1300–1361), one of the Dominicans' great preachers and spiritual directors, came from Strasbourg, had a profound christocentric spirituality, and was highly skilled in offering pastoral care and spiritual direction, mostly to nuns and beguines, lay women living together in religious devotion. He left us more than eighty sermons, a fountain of wisdom, and insight into his times. In one of his sermons, he writes about the wine cellar and how tempting it is to sneak down and secretly drink too deeply from the wine stored in the barrels below, out of sight from the public eye.[15] It is a revealing sermon about the culture and drinking habits at the time. He used this story to challenge pious groups that chased after charismatic experiences, getting "drunk" on them without maturing in their faith. Reform was always needed, and the ministry and sermons of German mystic Johannes Tauler contributed significantly toward the renewal of the church in the fourteenth century. His writings and christocentric theology profoundly inspired the young Martin Luther, showing him a path into a devoted life of faith outside the confines of monastic communities.

9

Martin Luther and John Calvin Sipped Wine

Now if we ponder to what end God created food, we shall find that he meant not only to provide for necessity but also for delight and good cheer. . . . For if this were not true, the prophet would not have reckoned them among the benefits of God, "that wine gladdens the heart of man, that oil makes his face shine."
—John Calvin, French Reformer[1]

The Decline of Monasticism, the Decline of Wine

The Benedictines and Cistercians, like no other monastic movements, spread throughout Europe and planted vineyards and crafted wine wherever they could. They settled along fertile valleys and hills and strategically used rivers and roads to develop extensive trade with the surplus of what they produced. These monastic orders were not just devoted to a religious life but over time became powerful commercial enterprises and trade brokers during the Middle Ages. Quite contrary to what Saint Benedict had envisioned for them, they worked themselves into becoming one of the most powerful and wealthy institutions of the Holy Roman Empire. A confusing and perhaps toxic mix of religious devotion, complacency, and the lofty heights of worldly wealth and power eroded the spiritual life from within. As these orders' wealth and power increased, their true mission to worship God, spread the gospel of Jesus Christ, and lift up the poor was eclipsed. Prophetic voices began to speak out against them.

In Germany, Martin Luther, an Augustinian monk, raised his voice and pen against the abuses of spiritual power within the Catholic Church, where a complex system of merits and indulgences put incredible pressure on the individual believer to achieve peace with God. He also challenged the monastic life and the vows of monks and priests as incongruent with the teachings of the Bible.[2] Luther attacked, questioned, and challenged monastic life to a fundamental degree because of how it was practiced at his time.

The peasant revolt in the sixteenth century, the Thirty Years' War in the seventeenth century, and the impact of the French Revolution all contributed to the steady decline and eventual downfall of monasticism. These events dealt an especially hard blow to the wine lands of Germany, because so many wars were fought on German lands.

The biggest blow came when Napoleon outlawed monasticism. By 1810 most monasteries and convents in France, Italy, and Germany were shut and their lands sold. The union between faith and land, earth and altar came to a grinding halt. Where once Saint Benedict envisioned the manual labor of the monks and agriculture as direct expressions of one's faith in God and in service of the gospel, this union was increasingly forgotten rather than reformed. Agriculture became a secular affair. The Reformers surely enjoyed their wines and praised them to the heavens, but agriculture was never their forte, nor did they seem to think it was worthy of or in need of much theological reflection.

Today, however, things are different. Thinking theologically about agriculture and how the Bible can inspire us toward the healing of the earth has become urgent and indispensable. We are seeing an unprecedented and rapid loss of fertile topsoil in which to grow food to feed the world. Will we still be able to grow food on these precious soils in fifty years' time? Soil scientists don't think so, and this is an existential matter for all of humanity. As Christians, we need to raise our voices against this exploitative approach to the land just as Luther raised his voice against the abuses and exploitations he saw in his own day.

Martin Luther and Wine

Martin Luther (1482–1546) loved good food, beer, and wine. Luther's contemporary Lucas Cranach the Elder, an artist, once painted a portrait of Luther in 1533 in which the well-fed Luther looms larger than life with a kindly and thoughtful expression on his round and full face. A copy of this impressive painting still hangs on a whitewashed sidewall in the small Lutheran church that I grew up in. I used to sit across from it and often stared at the features of this big man who had changed the fate of the German lands and eventually all of Europe in dramatic ways.

The Augustinian order to which Luther had belonged did not emphasize the importance of agriculture but focused on learning and study instead. His wife, Katharina von Bora, however, had been a nun in the Cistercian abbey of Marienthron, about two days' walk from Wittenberg, where Luther lived. She was well versed in the cultivation of herb gardens, agriculture, cooking, fermenting, and beer brewing, as one would expect of an industrious Cistercian nun. She proved to be an indispensable partner in Luther's endeavors.

When Luther helped Katharina and eleven nuns escape the nunnery, they found refuge in Wittenberg and married men of the Reformation, many of whom were former monks. It was a great scandal at the time, but once Katharina and Martin married, the Luthers turned the monastery in Wittenberg into their home and the happening place for the Reformation. It seems providential that Luther married a wayward Cistercian nun who was able to turn the former Augustinian monastery into an industrious Protestant household with considerable farmland, drawing on the agricultural wisdom of the Cistercians.

Under the oversight of Katharina, a new kind of spiritual household emerged, where Katharina became an industrious pastor's wife as she raised her family, cultivated a large garden, and added field to field to grow grains and plant fruit trees. She also brewed beer and cooked meals not only for her extended family but also for a constant stream of visitors, fellow reformers, and students. The Luthers also took in refugees, including orphaned children whom they raised in addition to their own six children.[3] Luther's famous table talks stem from those gatherings around the table, where they discussed theology while they ate Katharina's excellent food and enjoyed lots of well-crafted beer and wine.

When Martin Luther traveled and had to spend much time away from home, the Luthers wrote letters to each other. Many of Martin's letters survived, but sadly all but two of Katharina's were lost. Perhaps they did not seem worthy of preservation at the time. They would have given us much insight into her industrious agricultural work and skills and the seasonal life they lived. The agricultural vision of the Cistercians continued to live on in the life of Katharina Luther, nun turned pastor's wife, but was forgotten soon after her death.

In one of Luther's letters to his wife, one gets a glimpse into who Katharina was. Luther wrote, "You must wonder how long I am likely to stay, or rather how long you well get quit of me. . . . I keep thinking what good wine and beer I have at home, as well as a beautiful wife, or shall I say lord?"[4] As one can gather from this letter and many others, the Luthers had plenty of home-brewed beer and a cellar full of wine, and Luther enjoyed all of it with great gusto.

The Luthers received a large amount of wine as a wedding gift, and Martin Luther was paid in wine for various services, including his preaching, as was the custom at the time.[5] Luther drank wine daily. When traveling, he often missed the wonderful cuisine, well-crafted beer, and excellent wine that his wife provided at home.

It is said that Luther composed his now famous hymn "A Mighty Fortress Is Our God" while enjoying Rhine wine, one of the most popular and esteemed wines in the German lands at the time.

Not surprisingly, during the tumultuous time of the Reformation some people abused alcohol and drank too much beer and wine, and Luther condemned the abuse of alcohol vehemently. Some voices emerged that suggested Christians should not drink wine at all lest they are led astray and abuse it. Luther vehemently rejected this idea just like the early church fathers had done, and he proclaimed, "Wine and women bring sorrow and heartbreak, they make a fool of many and bring madness, ought we therefore to pour away the wine and kill all the women? Not so. Gold and silver, money and possessions bring much evil among the people, should we therefore throw it all away? If we want to eliminate our closest enemy, the one that is most harmful to us, we would have to kill ourselves. We have no more harmful enemy than our own heart."[6]

Luther understood only too well that a defensive attitude toward alcohol and life in general was not going to take care of the problems that arise from deep within. He had gone through his own turmoil and understood that freedom had to be wrought from the struggles of one's own heart.

Luther's desire was to see Christians set free so they could enjoy both God and the gifts that he gives so freely to his children, including wine. He thought that an overemphasis on asceticism and fasting could weaken a human spirit that is already tortured by guilt and shame. His pastoral advice was to make sure that those in bitter distress or under attack by the devil should be given plenty of food and drink and be encouraged to jest and joke, resting securely, as Luther wrote, "beneath the crimson tide of Christ's blood. Satan would have us wear black, but the joy of the Lord is our strength."[7] It is remarkable how well Luther understood the dynamics of shame and how it can shackle the human soul and drag it downward into a spiral of depression. He firmly believed that freedom can come only when one knows oneself to be forgiven and loved unconditionally by a merciful God. Therefore, Luther insisted that every believer should receive wine in the Lord's Supper and enjoy it freely as a gift from God.

John Calvin and Wine

John Calvin (1509–64) grew up in northern France in Noyon, not too far from the now famous Champagne region. Sparkling wine did not become popular until the early eighteenth century and really only took off in the nineteenth century. It was a cooler region and produced lighter and pinkish wines, made from the Pinot Noir grape.[8] The region lay at the intersection of two major trade routes, north-south between Flanders and Switzerland and west-east from Paris to the Rhine. Wine trade would have been a thriving business, with many abbeys cultivating vineyards and crafting wine. Calvin studied in Paris and settled in Geneva, both important trading places at the time. Geneva had a thriving tavern scene that Calvin sought to reform just as he had reformed the theology that had wrought so much havoc at the time.[9]

Calvin grew up and lived in a culture where wine drinking would have been more common than beer drinking. Though Calvin was deeply concerned about the abuses of alcohol at the time, he nevertheless celebrated wine and food as gifts from God that are to bring us joy and delight. In his *Institutes of the Christian Religion* he writes, "And we have never been forbidden to laugh, or to be filled, . . . or to delight in musical harmony, or to drink wine."[10] Calvin, like Luther, had a profound awareness of creation as a gift from God and that the role of food and wine went beyond mere sustenance into the realm of displaying beauty, delighting with their aromas, and bringing joy to our hearts: "Now if we ponder to what end God created food, we shall find that he meant not only to provide for necessity but also for delight and good cheer. . . . In grasses, trees, and fruits, apart from their various uses, there is beauty of appearance and pleasantness of odor [cf. Gen. 2:9]. For if this were not true, the prophet would not have reckoned them among the benefits of God, 'that wine gladdens the heart of man, that oil makes his face shine [Ps. 104:15]."[11]

Perhaps it surprises you to read such affirming musings from the pen of Calvin, who has become known as rather austere and severe among the theologians. And yet these lines show us that Calvin wasn't opposed to the pleasures and delights that God's gifts can bring.

Calvin's reflections on Psalm 104:14–15, "You cause grass to grow for cattle and plants for people to cultivate, to bring forth food from the earth and wine to gladden the human heart," bring his thoughts on wine to a climax. He writes, "In these words we are taught that God not only provides for men's necessity, and bestows upon them as much as is sufficient for the ordinary purposes of life, but that in his goodness he deals still more bountifully with them by cheering their hearts with wine and oil. Nature would certainly be satisfied with water to drink; and therefore the addition of wine is owing to God's superabundant liberality.... Bread would be sufficient to support the life of man, but God over and above ... bestows upon them wine and oil."[12]

What moving and affirming words these are. It is a grand vision of God's abundant generosity. For Calvin, we experience God's love, goodness, and generosity as we enjoy the fruit of the vine.

We have to remember that Calvin grew up in one of the most vibrant wine cultures of Europe and would have had a natural affinity for wine, which was then affirmed and matured in his study of the Bible. Like Luther, Calvin was paid in wine barrels for his sermons and ministry. He had a significant wine cellar to provide not only for his family but also for the extensive ministry of hospitality that helped further the cause of the Reformation. Theological conversations, discussions, and disputes around the dinner table were greatly enhanced by the home cooked meals of Idelette Calvin, who also oversaw the wine cellar.

Both Luther and Calvin gladly affirmed wine and food as gifts from God. They took great delight and pleasure in savoring God's goodness as they enjoyed wine with their meals and shared it with fellow Reformers and the community where God had embedded them. Though Luther and Calvin disagreed on many things, when it came to the gifts of food and wine, they were of one mind and spirit.

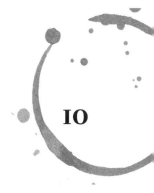

The Mayflower and
the Promised Land
without Wine

*Now the table was furnished with fat things, and with
wine that was well refined; and all their talk at the table
was about the Lord of the Hill; as, namely, about what
he had done, and whereof he did what he did.*
—John Bunyan, *The Pilgrim's Progress*

Just as Martin Luther and John Calvin celebrated wine as a gift
from God and affirmed its use in the Lord's Supper, so did the
Reformed tradition, more widely speaking, with Ulrich Zwingli
in Switzerland and John Knox in Scotland. Zwingli compared the
Word of God to a "good strong wine." He advised the young against
drinking too much but commended the use of wine in communion.[1]
John Knox enjoyed his regular glasses of wine and had an extensive
wine cellar. As was the custom at the time, he was paid in wine and

served wine to his guests. Knox, like all Reformers, affirmed the use of wine in the Lord's Supper.[2]

Given such a rich history of drinking wine among the theologians, when did the idea that good Christians don't drink wine slip into the teachings of church? What caused such a radical turn away from the teachings of the Bible, the early church fathers, and the practices of the early Reformers? As is often the case, there is a complex history behind it all. A particular set of unfortunate circumstances set the stage, especially in North America but also in Britain, for Christians to take a strong stance against the consumption of distilled spirits and eventually also against wine.

The Early Puritans Loved Their Wines

The early Puritans in England enjoyed their wines. Though beer and ale were the primary drink of the English peasantry at the time, hotels and wine taverns sold wine, beer, and ale to all who could afford it. Alehouses offered only ale and beer that had been brewed on the premises, and were mostly frequented by the poor, the unemployed, and, unfortunately, criminals.[3] Regular wine drinkers included the middle and upper classes, monks, and clergy. The wines were mostly imported from France, Spain, Germany, and Italy.

Before his spiritual awakening, William Perkins (1558–1602) used to frequent the infamous ale taverns and was known to drink heavily, not unlike many of his fellow countrymen. It was an alarming tendency in English society at the time, and the Puritans made it their mission to combat not only drunkenness and gluttony but also the plight of the poor.[4] Perkins became much more measured in his lifestyle and insisted that wine be used only in the Lord's Supper.

John Bunyan (1628–88) also affirmed wine as a gift from God. In *The Pilgrim's Progress*, one of the most popular books in the English-speaking world of the eighteenth century, he included multiple references to wine as part of the spiritual journey. Bunyan poetically muses on the use of wine in the Lord's Supper when he writes, "Now the table was furnished with fat things, and with wine that was well refined; and all their talk at the table was about the Lord of the Hill; as, namely, about what he had done, and whereof he did what he did."[5] Bunyan also believed that wine can bring comfort as one walks through life's humiliating valleys of suffering and disorientation. Like the Old Testament prophets, he saw wine as part of God's future redemption. In *The Pilgrim's Progress*, he envisions the heavenly Jerusalem, where wine will flow in great abundance, bringing delight to God and solace to pilgrims.[6]

Challenging Beginnings: *Mayflower* Runs Dry

The English Puritans, just like the French Huguenots and the German Pietists, celebrated wine as a gift from God and had quite a profound understanding of its purpose in the spiritual life. Rooted in the agricultural traditions of the Middle Ages, where monks and nuns had cultivated vineyards as part of their mission, the pilgrims now found themselves on new frontiers in North America. Could they, like the monks and nuns in the Old World, plant vineyards and craft wine?

The earliest settlers we know of who tried their skills at crafting wine were, perhaps not surprisingly, French Protestants (the Huguenots) in Florida in the 1560s, followed by Spaniards around what is now Parris Island, South Carolina, in the 1570s. They came upon an abundance of wild grapevines we now know under the name muscadine and concord. Thick skinned with insufficient natural sugar content and a musky odor, they weren't well suited for crafting wine like the Old World varieties that had evolved from the cultivated *Vitis vinifera*. Their sour taste and nasty smell could not appease even the poorest and least demanding of pilgrims. No further mention of an emerging wine tradition was made. Only in the nineteenth century did Americans hybridize the wild vines of the Americas with *Vitis vinifera* from the Old World and craft wines more pleasing to the general palate.[7] By that time, whiskey had already become the primary drink of the common people and profoundly shaped the drinking habits of the new republic.

The English Puritans had heard of the abundance of wild vines in the Americas and got inspired by visions of their very own Eden and dreams of economic independence from the French and Spanish. When William Bradford escaped to the Plymouth colony on the *Mayflower* in 1620, he saw wild vines growing in abundance in the woods around the new settlement.[8] Whether these early pilgrims had wine with their first Thanksgiving meal we do not know, though the *Mayflower*, a cargo ship, usually transported wine and dry goods. Their primary drink on the ship was probably beer and ale, staples of the English diet at the time. The English had little skill in crafting wine and sent word back to London to send skilled Frenchmen to help them realize their vision of a vibrant wine culture, but none were to be found, and the mission did not succeed. In addition to the lack of skilled vintners, they also faced the challenge of crafting decent wine from these wild vines. It was impossible. Uncounted attempts to plant the European *Vitis vinifera* on the east coast had failed because these cultivated vines did not thrive in the humid climate and withered away.

This was the fate of vine growing and wine crafting on the east coast of America from the time the settlers arrived until the nineteenth century. It created a void that needed to be filled, and this void was filled with strong spirits, first rum and then whiskey. Had the early settlers been skilled in hybridizing vines, the story of wine and alcohol in the Americas could have been radically different.[9] With no local wine supply, the consumption of wine became the privilege of the well-to-do upper class, which could afford imported wines from the Old World. Distilled spirits, especially rum, became the primary alcoholic drink of the lower classes and foretold an ill fate for Americans' relationship with alcohol.

Whiskey and Wine: The First Presidents Set the Stage

George Washington

It was a revelation to me to learn that both George Washington and Thomas Jefferson played a role in shaping the fate of whiskey and wine in America. George Washington (1732–99), the first president of the United States of America, had an important role in forging a path for whiskey, made from corn, to become the primary alcoholic beverage of the American people. Washington was born into a wealthy landowning family and enjoyed his wines, especially Madeira (a fortified wine from Portugal), claret (a French blend from Bordeaux), as well as rum and punches made from wine and rum. He learned from his family and the social and religious context of his youth how to enjoy wine and alcohol in moderation. He toasted with wine after signing the Declaration of Independence.

Washington had a significant wine cellar on his industrious estate Mount Vernon and brewed his own beer. He thoroughly enjoyed hosting guests and wrote, "A glass of wine and a bit of mutton are always ready and such as will be content to partake of them, are always welcome."[10] It was the custom to be served wine at Washington's table, preferably the one he liked the best, and he observed with diligence the rules of civility, which he had adopted from the French Jesuits: "Drink neither too slowly nor too hastily, nor as if gulping the wine, nor too frequently, nor without water—as drunkards do."[11] Washington insisted on a moderate, measured, and thoughtful enjoyment of wine and alcohol in his sphere of influence. After serving as the president, Washington withdrew from public life and returned to live on Mount Vernon, where he managed his extensive estate with the help of his Scottish farm manager, James Anderson.

I visited Mount Vernon not too long ago and it was quite a revelation for me to see what George Washington had begun, probably not realizing what a negative impact this would have on the future of the nation he had helped to found. This visit to Mount Vernon also made me think of Thomas Jefferson's comments on alcohol consumption in a new light. Thomas Jefferson understood something about alcohol consumption that George Washington did not. With few regulations in place regarding both the production and consumption of strong spirits in Virginia, there was ample freedom to allow the industrious spirit to reign supreme.

Washington placed his trust in Anderson, his farm manager, who had left his farm and distillery in Scotland to find new opportunities in the Americas without the incumbent tax regulations of his native Scotland on strong spirits. The Scots were heavy drinkers, and higher tax burdens had made it difficult to run a distillery in Scotland legally.[12] Anderson had all the skills and experience needed to build a distillery and make whiskey from corn, a commodity in ample supply. He advised Washington to start his own distillery on Mount Vernon and make a lucrative business out of it. And this is what Washington did. Quickly, they expanded the production to five copper stills and in 1799 produced 11,000 gallons of whiskey, which was valued at $7,500 at the time, approximately worth $120,000 today.[13] It was a lucrative business indeed, and George Washington became the most industrious whiskey producer of the United States of America at that time.

Apparently, many others in the state of Virginia drew inspiration from Washington. Only eleven years later, the 1810 census shows that there were more than 3,600 distilleries operating in Virginia alone. Significant technological improvements to the stills also aided this rapidly emerging industry. Rum made from imported molasses had been the primary drink before the American Revolution. Soon after it, whiskey made from locally grown corn replaced it. The appeal of a lucrative business must have removed any concern Washington might have had that the ready availability of whiskey and its abuse could have a devastating effect on this newly formed country.

Thomas Jefferson

When Thomas Jefferson (1743–1826) became the president of the United States in 1801, he had already been a United States minister to France and observed ordinary life in France during the tumultuous and violent period of the French Revolution.[14] He did not find the French to be a people given to excessive drunkenness. Perhaps it was his experience in France and the wine lands of Germany that made him write that "no nation is drunken where wine is cheap." It is an insight that is confirmed by current research of alcohol abuse. In Europe, for example, alcohol dependence is lowest in southern Europe, where wine is locally produced, inexpensive, and the primary alcoholic beverage of the common people.[15]

Thomas Jefferson greatly enjoyed his wines, had an extensive wine cellar on his estate at Monticello, and was very knowledgeable about wine.[16] All his wines were imported from the Old World. Jefferson had a great interest in horticulture and believed that agriculture was our God-given vocation. Unlike George Washington, Jefferson did not become a whiskey distiller and grew grains instead. He also invested great effort in planting vines in his native Virginia but unfortunately, as was the case for previous generations, had no success with it because of the unfavorable weather conditions.

Thomas Jefferson believed that it was important for a society to develop a healthy and constructive relationship with alcohol. He did not believe that distilled spirits or abstinence from alcohol were the answer. He wrote, "No nation is . . . sober, where the dearness of wine substitutes ardent spirits as the common beverage. It is, in truth, the only antidote to the bane of whiskey."[17] Jefferson understood something that Washington did not: he feared that the ready availability of cheap distilled spirits would not bode well for this young nation and its relationship to alcohol.

Jefferson had experienced a French culture where wine was affordable and the common drink of the lower class, and the French did not abuse it. This experience inspired him to dream about the lands of America covered with vineyards and wine as the common drink of ordinary citizens. It was a noble vision, but it did not become a reality, at least for the east coast. The west coast was a different story.[18]

A Downward Spiral
into Drunkenness

Repeated efforts by the government to impose taxes on distilleries and the production of whiskey to curb its consumption failed.[19] A tide of cheap whiskey rolled over the postwar lands of America. By 1792 there were approximately 2,600 distilleries operating in America. By 1810 it had multiplied to more than 14,000. And by 1830 it had increased to 20,000 distilleries, using surplus grain to boost economic output.[20] Production was also increased by the development of new technology. Between 1802 and 1815, the government issued more than one hundred patents for new distilling technologies.[21]

While the upper class continued to enjoy wine together with rum and whiskey, the lower class drank whiskey, and plenty of it. Heavy drinking became the norm. Whiskey was served in taverns, an important gathering place for the community. The golden liquid flowed freely at funerals, ordinations, military maneuvers of all kinds, political campaigns, and elections. Working-class people were often suspicious of the upper class, and politicians employed whiskey to level the ground and forge bonds of kinship with the lower class: by sharing a drink with the common folk, they sought to demonstrate their fraternity with them and their commitment to egalitarian principles. Even some clergy used hard liquor to lure the lost into their fold.[22]

The early nineteenth century was a time when America formed its national character, with many political, economic, and social changes happening all at once. The Revolutionary War had brought economic independence from England and its colonial powers. But the country needed to create new sources of revenue and develop political and economic alliances. There were a variety of challenges: rapid increase in population, ethnic diversity, the lonely existence of western pioneers, poor farm laborers, urbanization, industrialization with its factory system, and idle plantation owners.[23] And with these rapid and turbulent changes came a dramatic change in drinking patterns.

By 1810 whiskey, rum, and other distilled spirits became the third most important industrial product of the young nation. Can you believe it? The third most important industrial product! Never in the history of humanity did a nation produce this much hard liquor. It was a unique byproduct of the Industrial Revolution with its technological inventions. The ready availability of cheap whiskey, not surprisingly, profoundly shaped the drinking patterns of Americans. The consumption and abuse of distilled spirits rose drastically in the first half of the nineteenth century. It became the national drink and part of the American identity.[24] Alcohol abuse became rampant.

Prohibition

The consequences of alcohol abuse on American society were severe and threatened to disintegrate the American social fabric. This is when the temperance movement arose and gained momentum over the second half of the nineteenth century. The great American revivals made it part of their agenda, and the temperance movement became a Christian mission. It culminated with the ratification of the Eighteenth Amendment to the American Constitution on January 16, 1919. Taking effect on January 16, 1920, it forbade the production, consumption, importation, and exportation of intoxicating liquors in the United States of America. It lasted for only fourteen years, but its impact on North American culture was profound.

A vibrant viticulture had emerged on the west coast in the early nineteenth century, pioneered by Franciscan monks. As the century progressed, the wine industry in California blossomed and promised to become a significant cultural and economic force both nationally and internationally. But Prohibition brought this all to a grinding halt.

Additionally, Thomas Welch, a Methodist minister turned dentist, discovered how to pasteurize grape juice and keep it from turning into wine. This made it possible for the emerging evangelical movement to insist that grape juice, rather than wine, should be used in the Lord's Supper. It was a radical turn, unprecedented in Christian history. While Catholics, Episcopalians, and Lutherans continued to use wine in the Eucharist, evangelicals stopped drinking wine even during the Lord's Supper and developed a rather stoic attitude toward earthly pleasures more widely speaking. Alcohol, including wine, was seen as a snare that the devil used to tempt Christians into a sinful lifestyle.

Americans stopped drinking wine, and a whole culture was unable to develop a healthy relationship with it. Distilleries continued to operate illegally as moonshine spirits kept flowing secretly, hidden away from public scrutiny. Had Thomas Jefferson had his way, Americans would have had two centuries to learn how to enjoy wine in moderation and allow it to become a cultural force. But these conditions made this impossible. Prohibition was a dramatic turning point in America's relationship with alcohol, and even though the Eighteenth Amendment was eventually repealed by the Twenty-First Amendment in 1933, until this day America has grappled with how to develop a wholesome relationship with alcohol.

Despite this troubled history, since the 1960s, America has begun to develop a flourishing wine industry, and wine increasingly shapes American culture. It is now the most consumed alcoholic beverage after beer and distilled spirits. Wine continues to be part of people's faith, too, as they drink wine in the Lord's Supper and discover it as one of God's good gifts.

PART 3

WHAT WOULD THE SINNERS DRINK?

*Wine Poured Out in
the Lord's Supper*

The Jewish
Passover Meal

"Let the Israelites keep the Passover at its appointed time."
—Numbers 9:2

"This day shall be a day of remembrance for you.
You shall celebrate it as a festival to the Lord."
—Exodus 12:14

Blessed art Thou, O Lord our God, Creator of the Fruit of the Vine.
—Passover Liturgy

In this chapter and the next, I try to capture the history and significance of the Passover meal through an imaginative retelling of how Jesus might have experienced it growing up in Galilee, joining the throng on their pilgrimage to Jerusalem. I hope it provides a sense of how his life was embedded in the agrarian landscape and the religious traditions of his time.

Getting Ready for the Journey

There was such a commotion around the house. Mary was getting wineskins from storage downstairs, placing them carefully on the dinner table. She wanted to make sure they had enough wine with them to make this Passover meal an especially joyous and festive celebration. The Passover celebrations were always the highlight of the year as they took the pilgrimage down south to the temple in Jerusalem, but this year was different.[1]

Jesus was finally allowed to join his clan after watching them year after year set out for Jerusalem without him. He had heard of this pilgrimage all his life and could not wait to see Jerusalem. He longed to celebrate the Passover meal and the weeklong Feast of Unleavened Bread and listen to the rabbis in the temple. It was an exciting time. And rumor had it that God was on the move. The air was pregnant with expectation and there was excitement and hope that God had not forgotten them.

Joseph had gone out into the terraced fields surrounding the village to harvest their small plantings of barley. The sun had been warm and the weather kind. The first sheaves of barley were standing tall and strong in the field, waiting to be harvested to be offered up to God as the firstfruits. Jesus knew, like all Jewish children, that the family never used any of the new barley until they had offered the first of the harvest to God as a sacrifice.[2] The rabbis had taught him that all that the earth brings forth is a gift from God, and as they offered it back to him, they grew in gratitude and reverence for God and all that the earth brings forth. Ultimately, it was God who fed them with the dew of the heavens, the fatness of the earth, and the harvest of grain and wine each year.

The wheat always ripened later in the spring, and the grapes did not ripen until well into the summer. Jesus had already noticed the tiny buds on the vines that soon blossomed and flowered and eventually brought forth grape clusters. Slowly, the clusters ripened as the sunrays intensified in warmth, and eventually God chased the last sweetness into the grapes right before harvest time. He could not wait to help with the harvest and join in as they gathered at the winepress outside the town to stomp the grapes and watch grape juice flow down from basin to basin as if all the hills were flowing with wine. It was always such a marvelous sight and a joyous occasion.

Joining the Throng

They set out early in the morning. The donkey was loaded with provisions for the journey: the wineskins, the barley sheaves, and the one-year-old sheep in tow for the Passover sacrifice. All their relatives and friends from the village joined them as they made for the road down the hill country. They would be gone for weeks, away from their routines and released from the demands of their mundane lives, walking seventy miles one way.

The journey down to Jerusalem took them through rugged terrain. Others joined them on the road, close and distant relations, some old friends and many strangers, some of whom had traveled from faraway countries and brought exciting news from other parts of the world. With each day, the road got busier, and excitement grew as they shared stories and anticipated the celebrations and festivities. As they sung the Psalms, Jesus wondered about their meaning. He had only heard about these wonderful Passover celebrations, followed by the seven-day-long Feast of Unleavened Bread and could not wait to join in.

As they walked and talked and shared family news, they also prayed and practiced reciting psalms for the Passover. All the children had learned them by heart, and singing them with all the other pilgrims on the road was a moving and powerful experience. They sounded different, richer in meaning when they sang them together. One could hear them singing from the distance and feel the heightened sense of anticipation and expectant hope that had grown within the pilgrims. As Roman soldiers watched them process in such solemnity and joyful anticipation, they scoffed at these strange people and their customs. How firm these people were in their faith, keeping hope alive against the odds!

With great assurance the pilgrims passed by the soldiers. Hadn't Yahweh always been faithful to his people, and would he not act again? As they retold the story of the exodus and how God had miraculously delivered his people out of Egypt, would he not send an anointed one who could deliver his people once more? Sure, the Romans weren't as harsh as the Egyptians had been, but they still oppressed them with their heavy taxes and an enforced peace that wasn't bringing peace to them at all. As the years and decades turned into centuries, where was Yahweh? And how would he deliver them? Here and there some Jews had organized uprisings against the Romans, but to no avail. The Romans had killed them without blinking an eye. Now they carefully watched their step. Some of their own kin had become spies for the Romans, betraying God's people, bowing their knee to Caesar, not Yahweh. They didn't feel like they were a free people in their own land. Had not the prophets of old foretold that they would be a free people, each family sitting under their own vines and under their own fig trees without fear?[3] Would Yahweh not send another Moses and another Elijah?

As they neared Jerusalem, Mary kept looking for her relatives. It was such a thrill when she finally saw Elizabeth, Zechariah, and their son, John, join the throng of pilgrims for the Holy City. How much John had grown, and what a joy it was to see Jesus and John reunited after such a long time! Mary and Elizabeth looked at each other knowingly, pregnant with hope and expectations that others could not yet sense.

Jerusalem

The city was buzzing like a beehive. Pilgrims were thronging through the city gates from all corners of Israel. The temple was now in sight, and it was awe inspiring to gaze at it in all of its glory. The sound of the Levite priests practicing their chanting and singing was echoing through the streets of Jerusalem. What excitement, and what a special time it was!

On the fourteenth day of Nisan, the first month on the Jewish calendar, Joseph took Jesus and left early to go up to the temple. It was on this day that God had commanded the Israelites to slaughter their lambs in the fellowship of God's people, gathered at the temple.[4] The streets were packed with pilgrims bringing their sacrificial offerings to the temple. It was so crowded. Joseph was glad he had left early, the wineskin strapped around his shoulder, the sheaves of barley on his back, and the one-year-old sheep trotting behind him. As he carried these offerings up to the temple, Joseph prayed. He pondered that all of life was sacred, a gift from God, and offering up his firstfruits taught him that his sacrifices were a mere offering back to God what he had given Joseph in the first place. Joseph thought about the grape harvest last year, the first sheaves of barley he had just harvested, and the birth of the sheep a year ago. Gratitude swelled up in him and a profound knowing that without God's generosity, he could not feed his family.[5]

As they waited in the outer court, they could hear the blasts from the trumpets resounding throughout the temple area and Levites chanting the Psalms in great solemnity. It seemed ages before a Levite priest came up to them to receive their offerings. As the sun set, the priest took some of the wine and poured it over the altar. Another took the sheep and slaughtered it right as the sun scattered its last rays over the hills of Jerusalem. The sky was glowing with red as the blood flowed from the slaughtered sheep's neck. The whole court was full of slaughtered animals, and blood was everywhere. Water, gushing forth from natural springs under the altar, washed away the blood of the animals. As the blood mingled with the water, it flowed like the river of life from the Temple Mount down into Kidron Valley, bringing life and blessings to all of Israel. It was a stunning sight.[6]

The rabbis had taught Jesus that the essence of life is in the blood. That is why the Jewish people were forbidden to consume blood. It is the seat of life and belonged to Yahweh alone. All life comes from God and must return to him. As they saw all the sacrificed animals and all the blood mingled with the water gushing forth from God's temple, Joseph and Jesus were in awe of all the life that God had created. And this God, who created all of life, is the God who saved them. As the priests poured the blood over the altar as an offering, they trusted that just as God had saved their ancestors out of Egypt, so would he act once more on their behalf to deliver them. He would incline his ear to them, and they would call on his name as long as they lived.[7]

The Passover Meal

Mary and her relatives had been busy getting ready for the Passover celebration in the house. The table was set, the food was prepared, and they were waiting for Joseph and Jesus to return from the temple with the portions of lamb ready to be cooked over the fire. Plates were stacked with unleavened bread, several bowls with bitter herbs and saltwater sat on the table, and of course the cups waiting to be filled with wine.[8]

After they sat down to eat, Joseph read from the Torah as Mary poured the first cup of wine, the cup that speaks of joy. Joseph prayed, "Blessed art Thou, O Lord our God, Creator of the Fruit of the Vine." What a thrill it was after the long pilgrimage walk from Nazareth to Jerusalem to finally be able to sit down to celebrate the Passover, to remember and celebrate how God had saved his people out of Egypt and set them free! Yahweh alone saves, and in his love he commanded his people to hold festivals so they could joyfully live into their story as God's people. The past mingled with the present as the wine touched their lips and glided down their throats. Joseph continued to lead his family in the festivities and shared his reflections: "We will never forget Yahweh's great acts and joyfully celebrate our history as God's delivered people."

The wine is such an important part of the celebrations. Wine had always been a sign of God's blessing, and God gave it to them so they could celebrate and be glad in him.[9] When their ancestors were slaves in Egypt, they could not make their own wine and drank thin and bland beer, suitable only for slaves. But once they arrived in the promised land, they planted vines, and to this day they craft their own vintage. That makes them feel so very blessed and thankful, and it makes them hopeful for the future.

As the dusk of Passover turned into darkness, they awaited a new morning, renewed in their faith that God would deliver them once more. They took another sip of the wine, smelled and tasted its deep and rich aromas more fully. They began to feel the warmth of the wine in their bodies and a sense of comfort and relaxation set in. Their worries and anxieties seemed to fade into the background. For a little while, they laid them aside. The guests began to ease into the celebration.

Then Joseph took some parsley and dipped it into the saltwater and handed it to each guest. He prayed, "Blessed art Thou, O Lord our God, King of the Universe, who creates the produce of the earth." They chewed the parsley and tasted its bitterness intensified by the saltwater. They remembered that their ancestors were slaves in Egypt. And then Joseph broke the unleavened bread, and they ate it as the bread of affliction that their forefathers ate in the land of Egypt. It's hard to imagine how much they had suffered over the course of so many years in slavery, but the bitter taste and the dry bread sticking to their tongues surely helped them imagine how tremendous their suffering must have been.

Mary then poured the second cup of wine as Joseph instructed the children about this most special Passover celebration. The children learned that this night was different from all other nights. On this night, they remembered that God had passed by the houses of the children of Israel in Egypt when he punished the Egyptians for their great sins against God and his people. Jesus trembled as they carefully observed everything, and he wondered what this might mean. Had God not saved their forefathers, they might still be slaves in Egypt today. But even today many mourned and felt they were not a free people in their own land.

Then Joseph held up the shank bone from the sacrificed lamb and asked what was the reason for it. And all the guests joined in to answer, "Because the Lord, blessed be he, passed over the houses of our fathers in Egypt. As it is said, it is the sacrifice of the Lord's Passover, for he passed over the homes of the Children of Israel; he passed over our homes and did not come in to destroy us."[10] Then there was silence. Mary served each guest a piece of lamb meat, and as they chewed the meat and smelled its aroma, they pondered what it took to get the Israelites out of Egypt. It took a sacrifice. God had commanded the Israelites to take the blood of the slaughtered lambs to mark their houses so that when God struck the firstborn children of Egypt, he would "pass over" the Jewish homes and keep them safe. For the Israelites, life resides in the blood, and God forbade them to consume it because all life comes from God and belongs to God alone.[11] The blood on the doorposts was a clear message to them and the angels. The one who gives life is the one who also saves. God alone gives life, and God alone can save.

To ingest this wondrous reality, it took more than reciting some liturgically framed words. It took the slaughtering of another lamb with its blood splattered all over the altar in the temple court. It took gathering around the table and chewing, swallowing, and digesting its meat so they could ingest anew the hope that God would keep them safe as well. And the wine they drank, a sign of God's blessing and promise, lifted first their tongues and then their hearts to their benevolent God, who bountifully provided for them even as they lived under Roman rule. Their tingling taste buds sang of a hope that was yet to be fulfilled.

Sacrifice, Blood, and the Wine Cup Just for Elijah

"When you have eaten and are satisfied, praise the
Lord your God for the good land he has given you."
—Deuteronomy 8:10 NIV

Wine is very life to humans if taken in moderation.
What is life to one who is without wine which
was created from the first for his joy?
—Ben Sira, Jewish wisdom teacher

Some Musings on Sacrifice

I have always wondered about the need for blood and sacrifice. Why did the all-knowing God need blood on the Israelites' doorposts to pass by their homes? Was this a sign that God needed, or was it a sign that the Israelites needed?[1] And even more profound, why do we inhabit such a world where we have to kill in order to live? Why do we have to live by such a fierce exchange of killing animals to eat their flesh and live by it? Priest-turned-chef Robert Farrar Capon puts this question so well when he writes, "Red in tooth and claw, we come at last to a fierce and painful city, to the bloody, unobliging reciprocity in which life lives by death, but still insists that death is robbery."[2] It is a question worth asking. It allows us a glimpse into the depth of all that needs to be saved and redeemed, including the animals that we kill and eat. One day, so the prophets foretold, we won't need to kill in order to live. One day, as Isaiah writes, the lion will dwell with the lamb, and they shall graze together and live in a peaceable kingdom where there is no more death (Isa. 11:6; 65:25).

The etymology of the word *sacrifice* comes from the Latin noun *sacrificium* and the Latin verb *sacrificare*, meaning "making sacred." There are numerous words for sacrifice in Hebrew with a range of meanings such as "offering," "gift," "to draw near," "to approach," "to go up." What was once a common affair is now taken up into the sacred realm. The killing of an animal is no longer a thing out there untouched by God's grace. Through sacrifice it becomes a sacred affair, brought into the realm that belongs to God and exists under God's order. It gives dignity and new meaning to the cosmic cycle of killing in order to live. The God who created this world with its cycle of life, death, and new life is also the God who saves this world. The slaughtered lamb now represents God's saving acts. In the Old Testament, sacrifice was a vehicle of prayer. Through this act of prayerful sacrifice, the animals gained new meaning: creatures of God, given to the world and returned to God in gratitude.[3]

We see this cycle at work in the death of animals but also in the crushing of grapes and in the grinding and milling of grains to become wine and food for us. Sacrifice beckons us to reclaim the sacred nature of the world, including its cycle of killing and harvesting in order to live. God's salvation encompasses so much more than we usually envision.

We live in a world where we have been sealed off from this death-dealing cycle. We prefer to live in denial about it, but this is the world that God has made, and he wants to redeem all of it. To our late-modern sentiments, the idea of sacrifice seems offensive, and yet, as Margaret Visser wisely observes, we as consumers seem so unmoved by the cruelty to animals and to their suffering behind the scenes, hidden away from our sight. She writes, "Sacrifice, because it dwells on death, is a concept often shocking to the secular modern Western mind—to people who calmly organize daily hecatombs of beasts, and who are among the most death-dealing carnivores the world has even seen."[4]

There has never been a time in history when we humans, especially in the West, have consumed as much meat as we do today. And the way we raise, feed, and kill animals in our modern and "enlightened" world is devoid of any sense of the sacred.

As we ponder the meaning of sacrifice, suddenly we find new meaning given to this terrible exchange that has marked this world and our existence. We were born into a world in which life lives by death. We have to kill in order to live, and now God saves the world in the same way: life is saved by death, by the shedding of blood, by the life that God created in the first place.

God lifts up this cosmic cycle of killing in order to live and it becomes part of his saving act. Sacrifice is not cruel. It is a sign of hope in a world that lives by this "unobliging reciprocity." It calls us to be a community that looks for the redemption of all living things, even in the killing of an animal. The Passover sacrifice, the slaughtered lamb, is now lifted up and offered back to God. Those who shed its blood do so with a sense of awe and wonder for God and with respect and care for the animal that must die.

My husband and I no longer buy our meat in a supermarket because we know that the animals were kept in horrific conditions and died among the masses in inhumane circumstances to become meat for us humans. I know a local regenerative farmer whose Christian faith inspires him to keep animals with God's imbued dignity. The animals roam freely in pastures, and the cows eat grass just as God designed them to do (Ps. 104:14). The meat from these animals gives us the nutrients we so desperately need (think omega 3), and the animals die a dignified and sanctified death. We eat less meat because it is more expensive, but when we do eat it, we know that God's salvation has come not only to our souls but also to our stomachs, and not least of all to the animals that get to live in bliss before they die a dignified death and become food for us.[5]

Blood and Wine

The role of sacrifice also raises the question of the role of blood and wine in the Hebrew worldview.[6] They are profoundly interwoven. Since ancient times, blood and red wine were closely associated with each other, probably because of their similarity in appearance. The Jews sometimes called wine the blood of the grape (Gen. 49:11; Deut. 32:14). In the Hebrew Scriptures, God's judgment is at times compared to the treading of grapes in the winepress of God's wrath (Joel 3:13; Isa. 63:2–6; Lam. 1:15). As Jesus' family drinks from the third cup of wine at the Passover meal, they remember God's judgment but they also celebrate the redemption and new life that Yahweh has wrought for them.

Had he not brought them into a land of plenty where they could plant their own vines and craft their own wine? Had he not been faithful to them? Wasn't the wine they savored tonight a sure sign of his blessing and goodness, reminding them to take courage, to be joyful and of good cheer?

It is hard for us to imagine this, but for the Jews wine had an abundance of meanings, deeply rooted in their understanding of Yahweh as their creator and redeemer. They knew that Yahweh would not just stand by as the Romans continued to oppress them. They kept alive their hope in God, who would redeem them once more. With every sip they took, their hope was renewed as they tasted God's goodness in the blood of the grape.

And just as Jews understood blood as the center of life, so did they see wine as lifegiving. The Jewish wisdom teacher Ben Sira reminded his people of it: "Wine is very life to humans if taken in moderation. What is life to one who is without wine which was created from the first for his joy?"[7]

Wine had always been a tangible sign of God's blessing and therefore had tremendous spiritual, cultural, and economic value in Jewish life at the time of Jesus. It was common understanding at the time that wine stimulated the blood-forming organs of the body, and in Greek medical writings wine was a life elixir because of its healing powers.[8] All of these insights bear on our understanding of the Passover meal and, as we shall see, the role of wine in the Lord's Supper.

The Passover:
Monumental Experience

The Passover meal commemorating the exodus is a monumental experience for the Jewish people. Their identity is now marked by God's saving act. All of life is now reinterpreted in light of it. Let's ponder this for a moment.

On the night before the exodus, the night of the full moon of the vernal equinox, God shifts time into a new beginning. In his unwavering commitment to his people, he saves them out of slavery and makes a covenant with them. As his judgment passes them by, he leads them into the freedom of being his people. They now know who they are: God's people whom he saved out of Egypt. And they now know who God is: "I am the LORD your God, who brought you out of the land of Egypt, out of the house of slavery; you shall have no other gods before me" (Ex. 20:2–3). They have a new identity. They are God's chosen people whom he brought out of Egypt.

Their deliverance came at a cost. God bowed down to them and intervened and passed them by. This is no small thing. The creator of the universe stoops down and lifts them up. The one from whom all life comes and to whom all life belongs sees the blood of the slaughtered lamb on their doorposts and they are safe. By death, life is redeemed. It seems unfathomable. How can we ingest this great mystery? What celebrations can match the glorious splendor of God's merciful intervention?

The children who for the first time partake in these extended and magnificent Passover celebrations experience something awe inspiring. They never feast like this at home, and wine never flows so generously from the wineskins. What is the meaning of this? Why is everyone so very solemn and yet joyful? Why this abundance and generosity when for most of the year they eat and drink so simply and modestly? Something really great and amazing must have happened. The lavish feast speaks of it. There is so much to digest here not just in food but also in meaning. They need more wine as they commemorate and reseal God's covenant with them and strengthen their bonds as God's people.

The wine and the food are carriers of profound spiritual meaning. They draw the Jewish believers into a deeper understanding of their faith through feasting: as they smell and taste with their noses and mouths, they feel in their throats and bellies the goodness of their God who saves.

The Cup of Redemption

After all the guests finished their meal, Mary poured the third of cup of wine, the cup of redemption. As Joseph lifted up the cup, they all prayed from Psalm 116: "I will lift up the cup of salvation and call on the name of the LORD. I will pay my vows to the LORD in the presence of all his people" (vv. 13–14). Jesus took a little sip from the cup and drank the dark red, heavy, and fragrant wine, and he recognized it. It was the best of the last year's harvest. Joseph was very proud of it and gained some confidence that he too could make a decent wine with the help of his relatives. He had brought this particular wine to the temple to offer as a drink offering.[9] Only the best of the harvest was worthy of being offered up to God.

Jesus noticed the depth of flavor, the rich viscosity, and the savory tannins tingled on his taste buds as he moved the wine around in his mouth. It spoke volumes, and he swallowed it only slowly, feeling the wine glide down his throat like a warm blanket. He felt hugged and embraced and somehow more alive. And he pondered Psalm 116, and he wondered what it all meant: "Precious in the sight of the LORD is the death of his faithful ones" (v. 15).

The Cup of Praise

When Joseph lifted up the fourth cup of wine, the cup of praise, his family joined him in drinking it as they marveled at their God, who had created this world so beautifully, with the earth giving so bountifully, and wine flowing so freely: "Blessed art Thou, Lord our God, King of the universe, Creator of the fruit of the vine. You feed us with the fruit of your good creation. We will offer to you a thanksgiving sacrifice and we call unceasingly on the name of the Lord. Let us give thanks to you, O Lord our God, for the food and wine which sustains us every day, at all times and at every hour."[10]

Joseph then led them into prayers of thanksgiving for God's deliverance. Together they lifted up their voices in songs of praise once more: "O give thanks to the LORD, for he his good; his steadfast love endures forever! . . . With the LORD on my side I do not fear. What can mortals do to me? . . . The LORD is my strength and my might; he has become my salvation. . . . I shall not die, but I shall live and recount the deeds of the LORD" (Ps. 118:1, 6, 14, 17).

By now their celebration had gained significant momentum and a convivial spirit had overtaken the whole party. As they savored the rich wine and this special celebration, their hearts were touched, their spirits were lifted, and everyone wished that the feasting would not end, that they could keep celebrating into eternity. Jesus was deeply moved. He continued to ponder Psalm 118 long after they had finished reciting it. What did it mean that "the stone that the builders rejected has become the chief cornerstone" (v. 22)? He could not wait to go the temple to ask the rabbis about it.[11]

It was unusual for Jews to drink so much wine. Jews were not given to drunkenness. It was strictly forbidden by the Torah. Only during the Passover celebrations and other important festivals, over the course of a long night when they retold and relived the story of the exodus, did they drink wine abundantly, not to get drunk but to cultivate a deep sense of joy and gratitude. The four cups of wine highlight the extraordinary character of the Passover meal. The tremendous joy over God's deliverance must be embraced and cultivated and passed down to the younger generations lest they forget what Yahweh has done for them.

The Wine Cup for Elijah

Mary poured one more cup of wine, but this cup was different. They did not drink from it. Joseph explained that it was reserved for a very special time when the prophet Elijah returned. Whenever they celebrated the Passover, there was always an extra chair at the table and an extra plate and an extra cup reserved just for Elijah. Tradition taught them that Elijah would come again and announce the coming of the Messiah. As they opened the door and looked into the dark night, their hearts swelled with expectant hope and deep longing. John and Jesus looked at each other as they sensed a great bond between them. The season of watchful waiting had begun.[12] God's people looked into the future with hope and a great assurance that Yahweh, who delivered them out of Egypt, would act once more in the near future. Excitement was in the air that there would be a new exodus, where Yahweh would deliver his people from their oppressors, the Romans. Elijah's wine cup, filled to the brim, was a sure sign of it.

Wine and the
Lord's Supper

"Take, eat; this is my body," and of the wine he said:
"Drink from it, all of you, for this is my blood of the covenant,
which is poured out for many for the forgiveness of sins."
—Matthew 26:26–28

In this chapter, I offer an imaginative retelling of the institution of the Lord's Supper. Jesus is now a grown man, and he enters Jerusalem for the last time before his impending death. In this event, Jesus reinterprets the Passover meal in light of his own mission. As we will see, wine plays an important role in this significant moment.

The Beginning of the End

The atmosphere around Galilee and Jerusalem had become tense. Jesus' claim to speak and act on God's behalf had profoundly challenged the religious establishment in Jerusalem. Discontentment was everywhere, and the yearning for a new exodus had only increased over time. The religious elite, whose power base was the temple, had worked together with the Roman governor, Pontius Pilate, to keep any uprising in check. This was the peace of the Roman Empire: as long as there wasn't an uprising against the Romans' rule, as long as the people kept their mouths shut and complied, they were left alone, "at peace." Those who rebelled died a cruel death on the cross, the Roman form of execution. This public and barbaric form of torture and death worked well to deter the discontent and oppressed from any resistance or uprising. The alliance with Pontius Pilate had served the Jewish high priests and aristocrats well. It kept them in power, and it was lucrative. But now Jesus was challenging them and their claim to act on God's behalf.

Entry into Jerusalem

The time for the Passover was near, and everyone was on the move again. Jerusalem was packed, and the air was filled with both a sense of exhilaration and tension. Jesus and his disciples went to Jerusalem despite the increasing hostility he knew he would face. The crowds cheered when they heard he was near. They spread their cloaks and tree branches on the road, ready to welcome a king, when he finally entered Jerusalem on a humble donkey. And they excitedly recited from Psalm 118: "Hosanna to the Son of David! Blessed is the one who comes in the name of the Lord! Hosanna in the highest heaven!"[1] It seemed as if the whole city was in an uproar and wondered, "Who is this? What is the commotion all about? Are we finally going to see an uprising against our oppressors?"

When the time for the Passover came, the air seemed electrified. Jesus had profoundly provoked the Jewish establishment with his subversive teaching, pouring more coals on an already hot fire. He wasn't afraid of them like so many others were.

The disciples were busy getting ready for the Passover celebration. They had the wineskins, the unleavened bread, the bitter herbs, the bowls for washing hands. One of them had gone up to get the portions of lamb from the temple. A follower of Jesus from Jerusalem had opened his home, and they all gathered there for the celebration. They kept themselves under the radar, knowing how dangerous it would be if the high priests found out where he was.

The Passover Turned into the Lord's Supper

As dusk gave way to this long celebratory evening, Jesus, like all other Jewish hosts in Jerusalem, blessed and broke the unleavened bread and handed it out to his disciples. And then he took the cup of wine, blessed it, and passed it to his disciples. But the words he used were startlingly different from the traditional Passover liturgy. Suddenly these ancient actions, so familiar to Jesus' disciples, became imbued with new and perhaps even shocking meaning. When Jesus broke the bread and blessed it, he said, "Take, eat; this is my body," and of the wine he said, "Drink from it, all of you, for this is my blood of the covenant, which is poured out for many for the forgiveness of sins" (Matt. 26:26–28). The language Jesus uses is sacrificial language. Just like the blood of the sacrificed animal had to be poured over the altar, so now his blood will be poured out. Did not Isaiah speak of a suffering servant who poured himself out unto death (Isa. 53:12)? It was familiar language, but now it pointed away from the temple to Jesus. He now became the lamb of God that takes away the sins of the world (John 1:29; see also 1 Cor. 5:7).

But when Jesus takes the cup of wine and offers it to his disciples as "the blood of the covenant," he forges a new reality for his followers: Jews never drank blood, because for them it was the seat of life and belonged to God alone. God forbade them to consume it. Blood was a stark and consistent reminder that all of life belongs to God alone. And now Jesus invites his followers to drink his blood, in the form of wine, and ingest a new reality: Jesus is the ultimate sacrifice that will end the need for any further sacrifice in the temple. He now delivers from bondage and sin. And this sacrifice is not only for his disciples but for the many out there in the world, Jew and gentile alike. Now they drink the life that belongs only to God, and it delivers them and heals them.

The seemingly failed mission of Jesus, who challenged and opposed the Jewish leadership and suffered an excruciating and defeating death at their hands, becomes the cornerstone that now upholds and defines the very fabric of God's kingdom. His sacrificial death becomes the paradoxical key to the kingdom of heaven and the fullness of life on God's terms. By pouring out his life as a sacrifice for the forgiveness of sins, he becomes the spiritual food that brings healing and resurrection life to those who follow him. And his followers ingest this reality by drinking his blood in the form of wine. Just as it must have seemed paradoxical for his followers to consume blood in the form of wine, so did it seem paradoxical that Jesus' apparent failure, his death on the cross, became the only victorious path into God's kingdom. Paradox calls upon paradox as they ingest this great mystery by drinking wine.

Wine, Blood, and Jesus' Sacrifice

It's no accident that wine became the carrier for such profound and seemingly paradoxical spiritual meaning. The process of making wine parallels the process of how Jesus brings about God's salvation. Just like grapes must be harvested and crushed in the winepress in order for the grape juice to ferment and be transformed into wine, so do Christ's crushing death on the cross and his resurrection bring about deliverance, forgiveness, healing, and renewed life. The cruciform life is mirrored in the winepress. The prophets Isaiah, Jeremiah, and Joel even compared God's judgment to grapes being crushed in the winepress of God's anger (Isa. 63:3; Jer. 25:30; Joel

3:13; Lam. 1:15). Saint John picks up this powerful metaphor in his apocalyptic vision (Rev. 14:18–20). Christians throughout the Middle Ages, especially in wine regions such as France and Germany, saw and understood these parallels and visualized them in their art. Christ in the winepress is a powerful but mostly forgotten theme in Western art.

"Christ in the Wine Press," Hieronymus (Jerome) Wierix, ca. 1619. *Public domain.*

The parallels go even farther. We often think of God's forgiveness as something that happens to us as individuals, and we tend to focus on our individual sin and our need for forgiveness. But in Jesus' time, people thought about themselves much more as part of a community and understood sin as something that penetrated the fabric of the community and the society of which they were members. And God's judgment and forgiveness came to them not only as persons deeply embedded in tightknit communities but also as whole communities with all their structures and systemic sins that needed to be redeemed. Just as a single grape cluster won't be enough to make a bottle of wine, so forgiveness, though a deeply personal experience, won't work until Christians not only become reconciled with God but are willing to become reconciled with each other, especially with those who hurt us deeply and with whom we feel uncomfortable associating. It is not only relationships that need to be redeemed but also the social structures that we find ourselves in.

The way we live today, especially in the West with our heavy emphasis on individual rights and freedoms, makes it is easier to phase out those with whom we don't feel comfortable, who annoy us, who challenge us and wound us. That seems like a good way to avoid confrontation and pain, but loneliness and shallow relationships are the high prices we pay for it. The social fabric of our Western societies is brittle, often devoid of the rich communal relationships that only come from having endured God's consuming fire of forgiveness and healing together. When the grapes are gathered up and crushed together, their juices blend and are transformed into a cup of choice wine of Christian community.

And just as fermentation is a tumultuous, prolonged, and often tricky process that substantially transforms sticky and sweet grape juice into a beautiful wine, so is the process of receiving forgiveness and healing. It goes to the very core of our lives, where deep wounds and deeper scars, often hidden in our bodies under our skins, silently call out to be touched and healed.[2]

In Jesus' time and in the wider ancient world, wine was often used for medicinal purposes, and doctors would prescribe drinking moderate amounts of wine for various ailments. Wine was also widely used as an antiseptic to cleanse wounds. With its approximately 11 percent alcohol, wine was able to kill bacteria and help wounds heal. These physical properties parallel the spiritual cleansing and healing that happen in the Lord's Supper. Christ's blood cleanses us from sin and brings healing to our lives.

And just as a choice wine takes time to mature and evolve into something yet more beautiful, so does the healing of our lives and our communities. It takes great patience and a trust that time is a gift from God that works beautifully upon our lives once we have embarked on the journey of forgiveness and healing together. Maturity and wisdom in our faith journey are like a choice wine aged in God's wine cellar. In Proverbs, wisdom is personified as a woman who invites her guests to feast with her: "Come, eat of my bread and drink of the wine I have mixed. Lay aside immaturity and live, and walk in the way of insight" (Prov. 9:5–6).

In Jesus' time, it was common knowledge how wine was made and how precious wine was as a spiritual gift, cultural good, and medicine. Nearly every village and town had winepresses hewn into the rocks on its outskirts, and most everyone got to participate in the crushing of grapes, as young and old stepped into the basins and stomped the grapes with their feet. They would have watched with wonder how grape skins burst open underneath their feet and how the juice flowed slowly into the lower basin, gathering into a sea of dark grape juice. They would have patiently watched as the juice started to ferment and over time transformed into delicious and precious wine. Jesus' followers, familiar with the winemaking process, would perhaps have had an easier time ingesting his paradoxical teaching. His crushing death, his skin pierced, his blood flowing, an utter failure in the world's eyes, becomes the climax of his mission and the path to life in abundance. What appears to be an utter failure in the world's eyes is transformed into something so powerful and lifegiving that it is hard to grasp. The winemaking process hints at this great mystery in a profound way.

But the similarities go farther still. The crushing of grapes brings about the fermentation and transformation of grape juice into precious wine, a gift from God, a sign of his blessing that brings joy and gladness to his people (Ps. 104:15). Likewise, God's judgment and offer of forgiveness, if embraced with an open heart and gratitude, brings the kind of forgiveness where healing can flow freely and life can ferment into an abundance of rich and lifegiving relationships: with God, each other, and the created world at large, including food and wine (John 10:10).

How can we fathom such a great mystery that seems so contrary to our sentiments? It is tempting and perhaps our natural response to hide our sins and protect our wounds from further affliction. Jesus offers the beautiful and precious gift of wine as a way to enter this journey of forgiveness and healing. Once you ponder the winemaking process and watch grapes being crushed and transformed into wine, you might have more faith in this astonishing gift of forgiveness, where the healing of our lives can ferment into rich and lifegiving relationships.

Christ, the Noble Grape

"I tell you, I will never again drink of this fruit of the vine until
that day when I drink it new with you in my Father's kingdom."
—Matthew 26:29

Wine and Beauty

Since ancient times, wine has been considered a special and often costly cultural gift that elevates simple meals into something more festive. Wine imbues conversations with depth and inspires reflection as the savoring of wine stirs memories and evokes emotions within.[1] This is because a well-crafted wine, not the mass produced "two-buck chuck" from Trader Joe's, has a surplus of meaning. Wine can be utterly beautiful, express harmony, even exude something ethereal. The often subtle complexities and nuances in the aroma, the harmonious balance between acidity and sweetness, the interplay of fruit aromas with more floral or earthy tones, the alcohol that carries and holds and preserves these flavors and warms our bodies and changes our perceptions give wine the capacity to leave a deep impression on us. It can make us feel exhilarated as we experience such intense beauty not just with our eyes or ears. Wine has beauty we can touch, smell, and taste and is therefore a deeply intimate encounter with beauty.

Christ the Creator

In the Lord's Supper, the beauty in the wine speaks of our benevolent Creator God, whose nature is to give bountiful and beautiful gifts to his beloved children (Psalm 104). Up until the Reformation, the traditional liturgy of the Lord's Supper always included the following prayer, adapted from the Passover liturgy: "Blessed are you, Lord God of all creation, for through your goodness we have received the wine we offer you: fruit of the vine and work of human hands, it will become our spiritual drink. Blessed be God forever." This prayer reminded believers over and over (lest they forget) that all of creation, including wine, is a gift from God. The vine and grapes are often seen in the Hebrew Scriptures as the best of creation. This prayer reminded Christians that Christ the Redeemer is also Christ the Creator and that ultimately all that we consume comes from God and is a gift from God.

And this beautiful prayer celebrates agricultural work as a blessed and beautiful collaboration between God and farmers and vintners. It gives dignity and value to an "industry" that is often looked down on in our postindustrial technological societies, where being a farmer has little prestige. In the Bible, farming is viewed as one of our highest vocations as humans here on earth. When you hear such a prayer at least once a week, as Christians used to, it settles into the imagination and reminds you of the value and beauty of agricultural work and that real food cannot be manufactured but has to be grown in soil that we did not create and is therefore a gift from God. The psalmist put it beautifully: "You visit the earth and water it; you greatly enrich it; the river of God is full of water; you provide the people with grain, for so you have prepared it. You water its furrows abundantly, settling its ridges, softening it with showers, and blessing its growth" (Ps. 65:9–10).[2]

With the Reformation, this prayer was removed from the liturgy, perhaps because the Reformers feared it emphasized human work too much. I think it is time that we reintroduced this rich prayer into our liturgies to help us recover a more full-bodied understanding of God's work in the world: in the fields that our farmers sow, in the ripening of grapes that swell by the touch of sunrays, and in the magnificent process of fermentation, still little understood, where yeast bacteria work upon grape juice and transform it into something yet more beautiful and lasting. Vintners readily attest to the fact that all they can do during fermentation is be a kind of midwife to help ensure a safe birth. Humans can't "make" wine, they can only facilitate this magnificent process that God bestowed upon his good creation. I have interviewed more than thirty vintners and spoken to many more. All vintners but one, a professing atheist, felt that there is a profound spiritual dimension to their work in the vineyard and in the wine cellar that they found hard to put into words. Some even said that the Christianity they grew up with was by far too narrow to account for what they experienced in the vineyard. I think this should give us reason to pause and ask what version of Christianity they grew up with and why it could not allow the gospel to shed its light upon it.[3]

Christ the Redeemer

The beauty of the wine also speaks of Christ our redeemer. For those who have eyes to see, noses to smell, and taste buds attuned to the delicate flavors of wine, these experiences of beauty and delight can speak of the beauty of Christ's sacrifice. His sacrifice is like no other. Christ is the noble grape. Just as the best grapes are used to craft beautiful wine, so is Jesus the best and most beautiful of humanity—perfect and without blemish—offered for the life of the world. This is worthy of our attention and admiration. The choice wine at the wedding feast of Cana was such a wine and pointed to Christ as the climax of God's redemptive work. The sommelier at the wedding put it well when he exclaimed, "Everyone serves the good wine first. . . . But you have kept the good wine until now" (John 2:10).

Andrew Jefford, a well-known wine critic, once wrote about the wonder that he experiences when savoring a beautiful wine but also laments that as an atheist, he has nowhere to turn to express his gratitude. We Christians can learn to allow such a beautiful wine to help us ponder how precious the blood of Christ is that he shed for the sins of the world. It is easy to take for granted and not be touched by the beauty of a well-crafted wine or the incredible and beautiful gift that Christ's sacrifice really is. Beauty beckons beauty when a choice wine is served in the Lord's Supper and reveals the beauty of Christ's self-giving.

> "Everyone serves the good wine first. . . . But you have kept the good wine until now."
>
> —John 2:10

Wine and the Foretaste of the Heavenly Wedding Banquet

At the end of the prolonged celebration of the Lord's Supper, Jesus prepares his disciples for the time when he will no longer be with them. He gives them a glimpse into the unknown and offers them hope of a future reunion: "I tell you, I will never again drink of this fruit of the vine until that day when I drink it new with you in my Father's kingdom" (Matt. 26:29). It is a striking and perhaps surprising idea to us that Jesus prepares his followers for his departure by instilling in them the hope of a future celebration when they will drink wine together with Jesus once more in his Father's kingdom. For his followers, this would not have been surprising. The wine cup reserved for Elijah at the end of the Passover celebration had prepared them for the wine cup that waits for them at the end of time, when Jesus and the Father await believers with open arms, ready to celebrate. Other passages gather up the wine drinking into the vision of a full-blown wedding banquet for God and his people. In one of his parables, Jesus compares the kingdom of heaven to a wedding banquet (Matt. 22: 1–14) and an angel speaks to Saint John about those who are invited to the marriage supper of the Lamb (Rev. 19:9).

The Lord's Supper becomes the place not only where believers ingest the benefits of Christ's sacrifice but also receive the anticipatory joy they experience as they long to be reunited with Christ at the end of time. Christians are a people of hope. We believe that the future belongs to God and that Jesus will complete his purposes and fulfill his promises at the end of time, when he will judge the earth, wipe away all tears, and make all things new. Wine has an important role to play in helping believers cultivate this hope. Sacrificial love and the joy of our eternal salvation mingle as we savor wine. Wine is God's way of kissing humanity.

The Battle over the Wine Cup

Perhaps it is not surprising that this potent, powerful, and revelatory gift *and* symbol of wine should become the source of great dispute and feelings of ambivalence throughout church history, lasting to this day. As early as the second century, voices emerged that suggested Christians should not use wine in the Lord's Supper. I have already mentioned Saint Cyprian, who fiercely defended the use of wine in the Eucharist not least because of the astounding parallels between the winemaking process and the sufferings of Christ.

As monks and nuns, priests and missionaries spread the gospel in parts of the world where the production of wine was not possible, the question surfaced whether wine could be replaced with other beverages such as beer or rice wine. Upon reflection, the church's teachers insisted that wine had to be used to be faithful to the life and teachings of Jesus. After all we don't worship an idea detached from history and the particulars of place but a personal and relational God who knows, understands, and relates in the most profound ways to his creation. God chose to reveal himself in Jesus Christ, and wine had been a part of God's redemptive and revelatory purposes ever since Noah planted a vineyard. Wine found its climactic use when Jesus offered it as his blood to his disciples in the Lord's Supper. To replace wine with another beverage in the Lord's Supper is to disconnect us from the long history of God's chosen way of revealing himself to us. It would unravel the rich tapestry of the Bible and leave us wanting. We do not bend God's revelation to suit our particular and limited situations. Rather we are drawn into the particulars of God's revelatory world and have to find creative ways to connect with it. In the history of the church, this meant remaining dependent on each other. Churches in wine-growing regions would send some of their wine to churches in other parts of the world that could not easily access wine.

For more than 1,200 years the church faithfully celebrated the Lord's Supper with both bread and wine. In the thirteenth century, however, voices in the Catholic Church emerged that suggested that wine should not be offered to the laity. They thought it sufficient only to offer bread. It is difficult to reconstruct when this new custom became a universal practice. Independent thinkers and reformers in the free city-state of Prague, Bohemia (present day Czech Republic), such as Jacob of Mies and Jan Hus, carefully studied Scripture and challenged this new practice, arguing that it was unbiblical. Boldly, Jacob of Mies reintroduced the wine cup in his church in Prague in 1415 and refused to conform to the new teaching. He wanted to rekindle eucharistic devotion and preached that wine is an indispensable part of this sacred sacramental experience.

In June of that same year, the Council of Constance responded by officially abolishing communion with both the bread and wine. From this time the official stance of the Catholic Church was not to serve wine to the laity as part of the sacrament but only bread. This is still in wide practice today, even though the Catholic Church retracted its stance with the Second Vatican Council in 1970 and reintroduced the possibility of serving wine to the laity. I have yet to attend a service where this is the case.

Martin Luther (1483–1546) and John Calvin (1509–64) joined in this resistance movement and took Mies's argument farther: drinking wine from the eucharistic cup now became a defiant act to liberate the laity from the hierarchical and oppressive structure of the Catholic Church. The laity, as part of the priesthood of all believers, now became the priesthood of all drinkers: set free from the oppressive structure of the Catholic Church, saved from the bondage of sin, forgiven and justified by Christ's sacrificial death, they now stood before the living God free to drink deeply from the wine cup, where Christ, according to Luther, becomes truly present to them.[4] This powerful sensory experience was not to be withheld from ordinary believers, and both Luther and Calvin insisted that the Lord's Supper should be celebrated at least weekly, if not daily.[5] The power of God's forgiveness had to be tasted in bread and wine as often as possible.

It is striking to me that this rich and sensory experience should continue to be undermined once more, if not in official teachings, then in practice. I joined the Anglican/Episcopal church in my midtwenties, and one major reason for that decision was that the Lutheran church I grew up with served the Lord's Supper only occasionally, perhaps every six weeks or so. The Anglican church I explored during my graduate studies in Vancouver offered it weekly. It didn't take much persuading that I needed to taste the goodness of God at least weekly, and I have not looked back on my decision to become an Anglican/Episcopalian. And yet I see this reticence creeping in once again in various ways. When I attended an Episcopal church in Saint Andrews, Scotland, the priest insisted that the tiniest amount of wine, barely noticeable on my tongue, was all that was necessary to fulfill the spiritual benefit of receiving Christ in wine. Every Sunday I felt I had to battle for a substantial gulp of wine: the priest firmly holding onto the chalice and me wanting to get a good gulp to taste the goodness of God in wine. It was frustrating and spoke to me of scarcity and not abundance. Every Sunday, I wondered whether I would be able to get a generous taste and whether I would have to tighten my grip on the chalice to drink more deeply from the eucharistic cup. I was too stubborn to resign myself to a tiny drip of God's goodness and always tried to avoid receiving wine from the priest in charge.

More recently, I attended a class on the Eucharist in an Episcopal church. Receiving the Eucharist during COVID was a challenge, and the practice of dipping the wafer into the wine became the norm, though that is less sanitary than drinking the wine from the cup because of wine's antiseptic properties. As the priest talked about the Lord's Supper in a rather casual way, he did not explain the meaning of bread and wine at all and why it is so important for us to sense salvation. Instead, he emphasized that in the Episcopal Church, you don't have to drink the wine. It is not necessary for salvation. That was it. That was the teaching he gave. I never asked why he taught this way, but I wonder whether he, too, held ambivalent feelings toward wine in the Eucharist and the sacrifice it points us to. Our late-modern sentiments might find too much offense in it.

The drinking of wine is a powerful sensory and aesthetic experience. It has great potential to impress on us the mysteries of Christ's sacrificial death. A soggy wafer will not give us that powerful experience of sensing salvation as Jesus intended it. Perhaps it is time to overcome our ambivalent feelings or our urge to be practical or even worse to be stingy. Let us rediscover what it means to sense salvation.

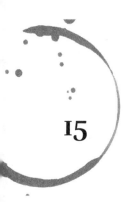

15

Sensing Salvation

Let him kiss me with the kisses of his mouth!
For your love is better than wine.
—Song of Songs 1:2

The number of tastes is infinite, since every soluble body
has a special flavor which does not wholly resemble any
other. Tastes are modified . . . by their combinations with . . .
other [tastes], so that it is impossible to draw up a correct
chart. . . . [W]e have been forced to depend on a small number
of generalizations such as sweet, sugary, sour, bitter.
—Jean Anthelme Brillat-Savarin[1]

Tasting Salvation

Tasting and smelling can and should be a profound and moving spiritual experience. The seemingly infinite potentialities of smells and tastes in our world and especially in our foods, including wine, are a lavish gift from our creator. God bestowed bountiful smells and tastes upon his creation and called it good. And he graciously has given us the capacity to sense them and take delight in them.[2] Our noses have millions of olfactory receptor cells ready to smell, and a human tongue has between two thousand and eight thousand taste buds. Each taste bud has between fifty and 150 taste-receptor cells ready to report to the brain, which is eager to be stimulated and inspired. Our capacity to smell impacts our subconscious long before it is brought to the cognitive part of our consciousness. Our senses of smell and taste are extravagant gifts to help us savor life as God intended it.

The whole world, according to theologian Alexander Schmemann, is presented to us as one all-embracing banqueting table, and this image of the banqueting table remains central throughout the Bible.[3] It finds its climax in the banqueting table of the Lord's Supper. Here Jesus celebrated with his disciples not with tiny wafers and even tinier sips of wine. Faithful to God's instructions, they spread a lavish feast where the senses of smell and taste play a central role in tasting salvation, experiencing God's goodness, remembering and celebrating his deeds.

The created world was always meant to be the place where we learn to commune with God, and feasting at the table is a heightened expression of it. Food and wine are not secular matter devoid of spiritual meaning. They are not meant to fuel our bodies as if we were machines manufactured for productivity. Food and wine are part of a great love affair between God and his people. As God's gifts, they are to nourish or bodies and our souls, reminding us of God's abundant love, benevolence, and generosity toward us. The beauty of the wine is meant to speak of the beauty that dwells in God, who gave himself so beautifully in Jesus Christ.

Never Taught

When we approach the Lord's table and receive bread and wine, how well prepared are we to smell with our noses and taste with our tongues God's goodness, to commune with God through the wine and the bread that we are to savor? How attentive are we to these spiritual gifts? The abundance and complex combinations of flavors in our world are an amazing gift and go far beyond the simple categorizations of sweet, sour, bitter, salty, and umami. These terms are like skeleton structures in the vast and majestic cathedral of smells and tastes that abound in the natural world. Often they are very subtle but nevertheless very potent. Do we have noses attuned to smell and tongues ready to attend to this incredible bounty?

Many if not most of us were never taught how to smell and taste salvation. We were taught only how to think and feel about it. We read about it, hear about it, sing about it, and feel about it, but to draw on our senses of touch, smell, and taste to understand and experience God's goodness? There is a long history to why we pay so little attention to these senses.

The Eclipse of Smell and Taste

In our contemporary world, so much of our food and drink is industrially processed by large corporations getting cheap ingredients from subsidized agribusinesses.[4] Think sodas laden with corn syrup or artificial sweeteners, corn chips, Velveeta cheese and Wonder Bread, and breakfast cereals covered with sugar and artificial flavoring and coloring. These are made from mass-produced monocultures, such as corn, grain, and soya, that have little flavor in themselves. The flavor is added in the form of fat, sugar (mostly corn syrup), and salt. These are powerful flavors, but they are monochrome, processed, and extremely unhealthy.

And the vegetables and fruits that are usually available in the supermarkets are also mass produced and tend to have little flavor or are overly sweet, such as apples and grapes. Carrots taste watery, peppers have no smell or taste to identify them, and tomatoes look perfect but lack flavor. More often than not, they also lack nutritious value as these varietals are winnowed out because they can grow fast and look pristine but aren't able to absorb the rich vitamins and minerals that a healthy soil provides. The nutritious value of our foods has been in steady decline for decades. We find ourselves in a culinary desert even as supermarket aisles promise an abundance of processed foods colorfully and creatively packaged to fool the eyes of the unassuming consumer. Processed foods and sugar-laden sodas have profoundly impacted our sense of taste and smell. They are loud and overpowering and have desensitized our noses and tongues to the more nuanced, delicate, and intricate smells and tastes found in foods that grow in rich and healthy soils, the wellspring of life, nutrition, and flavor. Mass-produced vegetables and fruits keep our expectations low: we don't even expect them to have any smell or taste anymore. Our brains are hooked on the addictive allure of high amounts of salt, sugar, and unhealthy fats.

It is an industry devoid of a sense of the sacred, geared toward maximizing profit, with little interest in allowing nature to reveal its astonishing beauty in flavorful food and fragrant wine. Theologian Robert Jenson puts it well when he asks, "How can we point our lives to the kingdom's great Banquet if its foretaste is spread before us with all the beauty of a McDonald's counter?"[5]

Even the flowers we pick up in the supermarket don't have a fragrance anymore. If you are lucky, they won't have any smell at all, but most smell of pesticides, which is rather nauseating and off-putting. Better not to smell them at all. Most fruits and vegetables in the supermarket no longer smell as they used to. Marketing experts understand that smell and taste are not priorities for us, so they tell producers to winnow out varietals that look perfect but have little to no smell. They are easy on the eye but disappointing for those who know that these foods used to be fragrant and full of flavor. The supermarket accommodates our preferences. Where do they come from? The problem has deeper historical roots.

Deep-Seated Suspicion toward Taste and Smell

The history of our relationship with our senses of touch, taste, and smell in our Western Christian traditions is complicated and has tended more often toward suspicion and even downright condemnation. Drawing on Greek philosophers, theologians in the Middle Ages such as Thomas Aquinas favored the intellect and the senses of sight and hearing. Aquinas even suggested that taste should not be considered as a separate sense at all. When it comes to the enjoyment of beautiful things, Aquinas argued that the senses of taste and smell have little to teach us. Here is what he wrote: "[T]hose senses chiefly regard the beautiful, which are most cognitive, viz., sight and hearing, as ministering to reason; for we speak of beautiful sights and beautiful sounds. But in reference to the other objects of the other senses, we do not use the expression beautiful, for we do not speak of beautiful tastes, and beautiful odours."[6]

These are powerful words, and they have had an even more powerful influence on Christianity in the West. Their trace can still be felt in our Western societies today. And I would argue that our reticence toward savoring wine in the Lord's Supper comes from this deep-seated suspicion buried in our collective Western imagination.

In addition to this, during the Middle Ages the senses of touch, smell, and taste came to be closely associated with two of the seven deadly sins: gluttony and sexual immorality. The whole framework of virtues and vices placed the believer in a struggle between gluttony and temperance. Eating and drinking, in this approach to the spiritual life, became a battlefield mined with temptations rather than an invitation to enjoy and savor God's gifts.

The biblical vision, however, is very different. Eating and drinking were always meant to be ways of communing with God, creation, and each other. Had the Christian tradition framed this particular virtue-vice paradigm more biblically, then believers would have been encouraged to cultivate the virtue of savoring, which includes temperance as a way to enjoy and delight in what God has given to us.

I regularly hold wine tastings as a spiritual practice, and I teach my guests that we should see savoring as a spiritual practice. But we have been trained for so long to focus on seeing and hearing that most guests find it difficult to pay attention to the more subtle smells and tastes found in beautiful wine. They were never trained in it and have little experience with it. They are desensitized to the subtle wafts of smells and the delicate arrangements of tastes teasing our tongues.

It takes practice and discipline to retrain one's brain to pay attention to what one smells and tastes. It calls on us to become quiet and attentive to delicate and subtle things. Just like the Holy Spirit often speaks to us in gentle whispers and intuitions that invite us to cultivate an attentive posture, so does a well-crafted wine invite us to become attentive and sensitive to its subtle and manifold nuances of flavors and textures. In our loud and fast-paced world, where our attention spans have been whittled down by social media, this does not come easy. It needs to be relearned. I therefore call on all believers to take more seriously God's invitation to savor the world, and this of course includes the gift of wine. Toward the end of the book, I will share some instructions for holding a wine tasting as a spiritual practice and creating a space for training up your senses to smell and taste the goodness of God in a beautiful glass of wine and a fragrant loaf of chewy bread.

Liberating News

It is a wonderful gift that anthropologists and neuroscientists have researched more carefully the powerful positive impact that the senses of smell and taste can have on our lives.[7] Anthropologists and sociologists have helped us see that food and wine are powerful ways by which we define our cultural identities and that we are socialized into our given cultures by the food and wine we share and enjoy around the dinner table. One cannot think of Tuscany in Italy without thinking of a Chianti Classic, or Burgundy, France, without thinking of Pinot Noir and Chardonnay, or the Rhine region of Germany without thinking of their Rieslings. These wines are part of these cultures' identities, and they have had an important role in shaping who people living in these regions are.

Neuroscientists more recently have added to these reflections with their research into the human brain. They have found that the olfactory cortex, that part of the brain that decodes the sensory perception of smells, is part of the cerebral cortex, which includes the limbic system, the layer of the brain responsible for thinking, perceiving, processing emotions, and forming memories, among other things. These different areas and functions of the cerebral cortex are deeply interconnected. The limbic system connects senses such as smell with our memories and our emotions. Smells can have a powerful effect on our emotions and the formation and recollection of memories long before we are even conscious of these smells. Think about the Lord's Supper and what implications these discoveries have for the way we remember Christ's death and ingest his forgiveness and healing.

Today, when we turn to wine experts to help us learn how to savor wine, they tend to rationalize the process of wine tasting. Perhaps this should not surprise us as this professional school has emerged from a decidedly Western intellectual tradition. They have been trained to focus on dissecting the flavor profile of a wine, where it came from, and what soil and climate the wine emerged from, whether it was made conventionally or organically, and so on. These are all helpful for learning how to appreciate wine. But this approach is by far too limited. When we enjoy a lovely wine together, the wine has the potential to call forth memories and evoke emotions, and these memories and emotions will shape our thoughts and conversations and stir our imagination. It is for good reason that wine has been praised and celebrated by poets and kings and educators. Wine has emerged out of cultures and profoundly shapes cultures and even civilizations.[8]

To Drink Is to Pray

Given all of this, it is time to reclaim the gift of wine, the gift of our senses of touch, taste, and smell in our pursuit of knowing God. In my German culture we have a lovely saying: to drink is to pray, to binge drink is to sin. When we approach the Lord's Supper, we should reimagine what it means to pray not only with our minds and our thoughts but also with our noses and tongues, and how doing so can evoke our emotions and stir them toward devotion. We should allow the wine to "speak" to us as our sensory impulses touch our emotions and stir our memories.[9]

The act of remembrance in the Bible and in the celebration of the Lord's Supper is not a mere recalling of intellectual ideas. It is a dramatic participation in God's faithful presence, recalling his faithfulness in the past, celebrating his presence with us now, and anticipating his work and presence in the future.[10] Fragrant wine, as it stirs our emotions and touches our memories, can help us enter this prayerful act of remembrance. As we sip from the eucharistic cup and smell the fragrant wine and allow it to touch our tongues, as we taste its rich flavor, and as the smell teases our taste buds, as the wine travels down our throats and warms our bodies, we remember and experience more fully what Christ has done for us. God's presence is rich, fragrant, beautiful, and lifegiving like a choice wine. So let us awaken our senses of touch, smell, and taste so we can sense more profoundly God's redeeming presence in our midst. To drink is to pray.

PART 4

WHY SOME NEED NOT DRINK

*Abuses, Addictions,
and the Call to Healing*

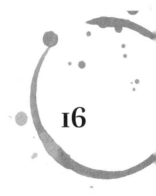

Wine Use and Abuse in the Bible

Hear, my child, and be wise, and direct your mind in the
way. Do not be among the winebibbers or among gluttonous
eaters of meat, for the drunkard and the glutton will come
to poverty, and drowsiness will clothe them with rags.
—Proverbs 23:19–21

Different Times, Different Challenges

The Bible affirms wine as a gift from God that is to bring gladness to our hearts and enhance our festive play before God. It should not surprise us that it also addresses the abuse of wine and condemns drunkenness and wine abuse throughout its narrative.

The biblical context, however, is vastly different from our times, and we have to contend with much more challenging questions today. A major difference between biblical times and our time is the ready availability today of a wide range of alcoholic beverages and especially distilled spirits. Hard liquor, as we rightly call it, is much higher in alcohol content than wine and is offered to us in endless forms and combinations. It is much easier to get intoxicated by consuming seemingly small amounts of hard liquor than by wine. There is little cultural awareness that tells us that perhaps we need to be more cautious with it.

There is indeed a difference between sipping a glass of wine and drinking a shot or two of bourbon or whiskey on the rocks, rum in a mojito cocktail, tequila in a margarita, or vodka in a Bloody Mary. In cocktails one doesn't even notice the alcohol much and the added sugar heightens alcohol's impact on the body. Cocktails glide down like a glass of lemonade. It is only after one gets up that one suddenly realizes how intoxicating these mixed drinks are. It takes much more wisdom and insight into today's techno-industrialized and highly lucrative alcohol industry to understand that we are fighting a rather different animal than did the pilgrims of biblical times, when most families produced small batches of wine for their own consumption.

Different Times

You might not know this but in biblical times, alcohol distilleries did not exist and no one had access to hard liquor. It was only with the Industrial Revolution that distilleries were built on a mass scale and produced vast amounts of distilled spirits. Beginning in the nineteenth century in the United Kingdom and the Americas, distilled spirits, much higher in alcohol than wine, became a primary drink among the common people, and this is still true today. I have often been surprised to see how much more popular distilled spirits are in North America than in Europe, especially in countries with a thriving wine industry such as France, Spain, Italy, and Germany.

In biblical times the primary mode of transportation was walking, while today most of us drive a car, and the dangers that have come with drunk driving cannot be overestimated. Another difference is that society was much more cohesive than it is today. We live in times of profound cultural, social, and political turmoil and friction, with few shared values and common goals that unite us. Our societies are highly competitive and individualistic, with incredible pressures on individuals to perform and even outperform their peers. In biblical times, people drank together during family meals and in various social and religious gatherings. Today, too many drink alone, be it in the secrecy of their home or as lone rangers at bars.[1] Alcohol, as a consumer product, plays an important role in this system as it promises easy and readily available relief from these complex pressures. Many turn to alcoholic beverages to find relaxation and comfort after a busy and demanding day at work, in the midst of stressful situations in family life, or in social groups defined by what members consume rather than the values they share.

In the biblical account, however, wine is not understood as a consumer product. People did not walk into a wine bar after a stressful day at work or mix themselves a cocktail to leave behind the stresses and worries of the day. Wine bars and pubs, liquor stores, and wine shops and restaurants did not exist. In the Bible, wine is understood as a divine gift meant to enrich and strengthen spiritual, communal, and agricultural ties. Children were socialized into drinking wine through regular participation in religious rituals such as the weekly Sabbath. In biblical times, wine was produced on small family farms and was always shared in the family context, and drinking was closely monitored by the cultural norms at play in these social gatherings. Wine was drunk in the context of family meals, feasts, and celebrations. In these intimate gatherings, trust and loyalty opened up a social space to relax and be refreshed, to allow a festive and convivial spirit to bring ease, merriment, and deeper communal bonding. Though these occasions and the underlying trust were at times abused, such occasions of drunkenness served to reinforce biblical ideals and religious and social norms rather undermine them.[2]

Merriment and Holy Tipsiness

What strikes me as noteworthy about intoxication in the Bible is the awareness of the different levels of intoxication that can happen when wine flows generously and freely. Not all intoxication is seen as negative, and the Bible speaks freely about the positive effects of a slight level of intoxication. Psalm 104:15 specifically emphasizes that wine is supposed to add an extra level of gladness and merriment to our lives. I call this holy intoxication. This slight level of intoxication allows merriment and gladness to gain momentum and create a special kind of openness and trust where guests share more freely and vulnerably and, because of it, a deeper bonding can happen among the guests. It strengthens one's sense of belonging as joyous celebrations seal bonds of kinship and friendship. The prophet Zechariah even compares the gladness that God's deliverance brings to his people to the gladness that wine can bring to our hearts (Zech. 10:7). Certainly, the guests at the wedding feast of Cana were not rebuked for their state of intoxication (John 2:10). It seems appropriate for the wonderful wedding festivities that not only celebrated the couple's marriage in the context of God's covenant faithfulness but also forged stronger bonds of kinship and friendship among the new families being brought together through this marriage.

When people are too reserved, it is too easy not to open up, not to trust, not to become vulnerable and share things that could move a gathered group to a deeper sense of knowing and communing with each other. In German, we even have a word for people who are not willing to show emotions, who are always matter of fact and unable or unwilling to be vulnerable and open up in a group setting. We call them "sober," and it is not a compliment. To become open, trusting, and vulnerable always includes risk, but the call to love each other invites us to this deeper, more trusting, and more vulnerable way of knowing and bonding with each other. That these trusting communal and celebratory experiences can be misused and abused should not surprise us. The Bible has plenty of stories that narrate such a betrayal of trust.

Drunkenness and the
Betrayal of Trust

One level of drunkenness that the Bible explores frequently is occasional drunkenness. Though the Bible does not seem to condemn it, the consequences of vulnerability, being incapacitated, and the potential betrayal of trust serve as a severe warning. The story of Noah's drunkenness is the first of its kind. Noah is the first person in the Bible to plant a vineyard and enjoy wine and, perhaps not surprisingly, gets intoxicated to such an extent that it incapacitates him. He falls asleep naked in his tent rather than properly clothing himself for the night. His son Ham stumbles into the tent, and instead of covering up his father and protecting his reputation, he spreads the embarrassing news to the wider public and brings great shame upon his father, compromising his reputation (Gen. 9:20–25).[3]

The story of Lot and his daughters is another example. Two daughters get their father drunk with wine and incapacitated in order to sleep with him and secure for themselves descendants. It is to us an abhorrent story of incest, raw calculation, and the abuse of family trust. I often wonder what the alternative would have been for Lot's refugee daughters (Gen. 19:32–38).

Jacob does not even notice that he spent his wedding night with the wrong person, and he wakes up to grave disappointment when he finds Leah and not Rachel beside him in the morning. His father-in-law, Laban, surely took advantage of the wedding festivity with its implied trust and benevolence. As wine flowed freely and Jacob's senses dulled, he trusted too much in Laban's good will toward him. Laban, more mindful of his need to marry off his oldest daughter first, smuggled Leah into the nuptial chamber and caught Jacob off guard. It is a tragic story (Genesis 29). Jacob himself had tricked his own father with food, and the abuse of trust around meals caught up with him (Genesis 27).

In 1 Kings 16 we learn of Elah, the king of Israel, who is murdered in a military coup. He had entrusted his servant Zimri with the command of half of his military. Little did he know that Zimri was waiting for an opportunity to overturn his rule. One day Zimri finds

King Elah drunk at a banquet in Tirzah and seizes the opportunity to strike him down and take the throne (1 Kings 16:8–10). It is no wonder that Proverbs advises kings and rulers to refrain from drinking wine and intoxicating drink; it is just too risky (Prov. 31:4–5, 8–9).

King David, after raping his servant Uriah's wife, Bathsheba, schemes to get Uriah drunk in order to cover up the unwanted pregnancy, but Uriah innocently and unknowingly resists David's schemes. In the end David sends Uriah to his death in the battlefield. David had wanted to betray the loyalty of one of his most faithful servants, weaponizing wine and drunkenness against Uriah, but without success (2 Sam. 11:2–13).[4] This story shows how even God's very own people will turn his precious gifts into weapons to cover up their depraved desires. The Bible warns against weaponizing wine and yet consistently upholds wine as God's gift to bring joy and peace. Isaiah puts it beautifully when he speaks of God's redemption, when weapons of war will be turned into pruning hooks, knives especially made for pruning vines toward fruitfulness (Isa. 2:4).

When Jesus celebrates the Passover meal with his disciples, this intimate sharing of wine and bread, roasted lamb and prayers with his beloved disciples also becomes the occasion when Judas's betrayal is revealed: "It is the one to whom I give this piece of bread when I have dipped it in the dish" (John 13:26). Jesus does not refuse to share bread and wine with those who will later betray him. The risk of love and the beauty of the table will not keep at bay those whose hearts are set on betrayal, but Jesus invites us to keep the feast in spite of them.

Habitual Drunkenness

Perhaps the strongest rebuke against the abuse of wine comes to those who abuse it habitually. The book of Proverbs, written to young people learning the ways of wisdom, pays significant attention to habitual wine abuse and even describes vividly the state of severe drunkenness and the hangover that follows it: "Who has woe? Who has sorrow? Who has strife? Who has complaining? . . . Those who linger late over wine, those who keep trying mixed wines. Do not look at wine when it is red, when it sparkles in the cup and goes down smoothly. At the last it bites like a serpent and stings like an adder. Your eyes will see strange things, and your mind utter perverse things. You will be like one who lies down in the midst of the sea, like one who lies on the top of a mast" (Prov. 23:29–34).

While a slight sense of intoxication can heighten one's awareness of reality and open one up to meaningful conversations and strengthen communal bonding, heavy drinking and severe drunkenness do the opposite: they decapacitate a person from functioning properly and impair one's senses. They help unleash abusive and offensive behavior, destroying bonds of love and respect in the face of excessive and uncontrolled drinking. For this the Bible has clear and consistent words: stay away from it.[5]

The prophet Isaiah rebukes wealthy rulers who amass possessions and oppress the poor and spend entire days indulging in wine, feasting to excess (Isa. 5:8–12; 28:1, 3). The apostle Paul, who ministered in pagan contexts where drunkenness was often permissible or even encouraged, has little patience with it. He admonishes a group of older women on the island of Crete to give up heavy drinking and practice moderation instead (Titus 2:3). He challenges the believers in Galatia to stay away from drunkenness (Gal. 5:19–21) and even encourages the church in Corinth repeatedly to stay away from those given to alcohol abuse (1 Cor. 5:11; 6:10).

Though we have only touched on a few passages, it is clear that the Bible condemns alcohol abuse and drunkenness and instead encourages a wise and wholesome consumption of wine. It is noteworthy that the book of Proverbs frames its discussion of alcohol abuse with three positive affirmations of wine as a gift from God. One at the beginning and two at the end (Prov. 3:10; 31:6, 16). Climactically, wisdom is even compared to a wife who plants a vineyard and by doing so invests in God's future.

17

Moonshine Hangover

Wine was given to make us cheerful, not to make us
behave shamefully; to make us laugh, not a laughing
stock; to make us healthy, not sick; to mend the
weakness of the body, not to undermine the soul.
—Saint John Chrysostom[1]

Rum Runners and Moonshiners

My husband and I recently visited Uncle Tom, my husband's ninety-one-year-old uncle, who lives in the Appalachian Mountains. We live right along the foothills of the Appalachians in Birmingham, Alabama, but the scenery around Uncle Tom's home in North Wilkesboro, near the Blue Ridge Parkway, is breathtaking. Uncle Tom is the only family member on my husband's side of the family to have tried his hand on wine crafting and still has a few bottles of his own wine sitting in his wine cellar. It was an odd thing to do in the Appalachian Mountains twenty years ago, but then, Uncle Tom is no run-of-the-mill Southerner.

The Appalachian Mountains are best known for their moonshiners. The history of moonshine spirits (illegally produced and sold distilled spirits) goes back to Scots-Irish settlers who brought their distilling skills with them and is deeply entrenched in Southern culture.[2] With the Prohibition, which officially started on January 16, 1920, the production of whiskey became illegal but continued to flourish illegally in many parts of the South. Southerners were only too eager to defy the government. After all, the wounds of the Civil War, which officially ended in 1865, were still fresh, burning with a spirit of defiance.

Rum runners in Louisiana took advantage of the marshlands to hide their operations and smuggled their whiskey into New Orleans via the Mississippi River. New Orleans had been a flourishing port city, with rum and whiskey being imported from South America and the Caribbean. With Prohibition, these operations did not stop but went underground and flourished illegally. Corruption and crime became the norm in order to outwit the federal government.

The moonshiners of the Appalachians took to a different strategy to outpace their revenuers, as they called them—government officials trying to confiscate illegally produced whiskey. Uncle Tom had many stories to tell, but one of the most fascinating ones for me was the history of NASCAR auto racing. Moonshiners used winding and sometimes treacherous back roads to escape the revenuers who chased after them. To make their cars faster, the moonshiners souped up the engines of their cars, often a '35 Ford, to outrun government officials. They became experts at navigating narrow roads and tight turns. Eventually, they turned these races into a pastime, and NASCAR is a direct outcome of it. I had no idea!

One cannot imagine the history of the South, and the US more widely speaking, without these stories of moonshine operations. I first learned of them when I read the enchanting story *The Education of Little Tree* by Forrest Carter, in which Cherokee grandparents of Little Tree are accused of being unfit guardians because Grandpa has a criminal record for making moonshine. It is a beautifully haunting story of how complex the issues around moonshine production really were and how important moonshine was to boost the livelihoods of poor people.

The South is changing, though, and the little town of North Wilkesboro, where Uncle Tom lives, now holds an annual festival called From Shine to Wine, celebrating wine as a new addition to Appalachia's evolving culture. The first festival featured retired moonshiners and revenuers telling their stories of chasing each other up and down the Appalachian Mountains.

Moonshine Trauma

One of the readily accessible articles on the history of moonshine was published by the Oxford Treatment Center, part of the American Addiction Centers, a nationwide network of addiction rehab facilities. They offer help to those caught in the perilous claws of alcohol and drug addiction. Even though the history of moonshine is an entertaining story to tell, with a reality TV series called *Moonshiners* celebrating the production of moonshine whiskey as a fascinating part of Southern culture, it is a deeply ambivalent part of American history, reaching back to America's very inception.

The first European settlers saw wine and beer as staples and brought plenty of it with them. By the time the *Mayflower* arrived in the Americas, the thirsty pilgrims had consumed nearly all of the beer on board before they set foot on land. Future immigrants came better prepared. When the Puritans set sail on the *Arbella* in 1630, they carried ten thousand gallons of wine and three times more beer than water.[3] Of course these supplies did not last. Many a European settler tried to plant vineyards with vines they brought from Europe, but these European varietals did not flourish on the eastern shores of the Americas because of unfavorable weather conditions. This unfortunate historical viticultural circumstance shaped the drinking habits of Americans for centuries to come.[4]

Colonial entrepreneurs saw the demand for alcohol and began a thriving rum trade with the West Indies. They also started to make apple cider. Distilled spirits, including whiskey, rum, gin, and brandy, became the primary alcoholic beverage, together with hard cider. Americans became known as heavy habitual drinkers and developed a high degree of tolerance for alcohol. Alcohol consumption decreased after the Revolution because of high import duties on West Indian rum and a new tax on domestic whiskey. However, with prosperity, improved distilling technology, and the growing popularity of whiskey, whether legally or illegally produced, per capita consumption skyrocketed in the early nineteenth century. Historian W. J. Rorabaugh carefully shows that alcohol consumption increased dramatically between 1800 to 1830 and exceeded five gallons of pure alcohol per person per year.[5] Today Americans consume less than two gallons of pure alcohol a year, mostly in the form of beer, then distilled spirits, followed by wine.

What makes this particular history so difficult is that it wasn't just entrepreneurs but the first president of the United States, George Washington, who took the production of whiskey to an unprecedented scale. Let's pause here for a moment to ponder this: Upon retiring from his office as president in 1797, Washington withdrew to his Mount Vernon estate and, together with his Scottish estate manager, James Anderson, built the largest distillery in the country, and it became the most profitable enterprise of his estate. Any moral concerns that he might have had were certainly lost in this particular enterprise. Washington's industrious spirit inspired the rest of the state, and by 1810 there were more than 3,600 distilleries operating in Virginia. Temperance historian Daniel Dorchester records that in 1792, the United States had 2,579 distilleries, and by 1820 there were 14,191 distilleries officially operating.[6] This does not include undocumented moonshine distilleries, including the ones that Scots-Irish immigrants were operating in the Appalachian Mountains at the time. Whiskey rather than wine became the primary drink of the common people.[7] Americans, including women and children, drank on all occasions and, as Rorabaugh put it, enjoyed a "spectacular binge." Between 1800 and 1830, the annual per capita consumption increased to more than five gallons, or nineteen liters.[8]

The destruction that this "spectacular binge" brought to families and communities was horrendous. Domestic violence, economic ruin, and widespread criminal behavior were common. Women and children suffered the most as fathers became addicted and could not care for their families. A broadside published by the temperance movement called "The Drunkard's Progress, or the Direct Road to Poverty, Wretchedness and Ruin," published in 1826, vividly depicts the downfall of an American family as the father's addiction to alcohol ruins the family estate.[9]

> Wine was given to make us cheerful, not to make us behave shamefully; to make us laugh, not a laughing stock; to make us healthy, not sick; to mend the weakness of the body, not to undermine the soul.
>
> —Saint John Chrysostom

The American Prohibition pushed whiskey production underground, alcohol was consumed more secretly, away from public scrutiny, and the budding wine culture in California came to a screeching halt. As a society, Americans were not able to evolve and develop a more wholesome drinking culture. Since the country did not have its own viticulture and had to import wine for the upper class, there was no understanding among the general population that wine paired with food and enjoyed around the dinner table had been a powerful cultural force for many great civilizations, including Europe.

Strong spirits remained the primary drink of the common people, and the illegal production of moonshine spirits continued to flourish. The tensions between the North and the South, climaxing in the Civil War, only exacerbated things, and alcohol abuse continued to be widespread, traumatizing generations to come, especially in the South. This trauma many born-again evangelical Christians brought with them into their faith communities. As we learn more about trauma and how it haunts us, it is no longer surprising to me that those affected by alcohol abuse cannot fathom and rationally engage with arguments that wine in the Bible had alcohol in it and was not in fact just grape juice. I have had many a conversation with believers in the South in which I became very aware that what was most needed was not a well-substantiated argument about the biblical, archaeological, and historical facts on wine but a pastoral response to believers who have lived with considerable trauma all of their lives because of family members suffering from addiction. Moonshine hangover settled deeply into the American soul and continues to linger.

18

Some Sobering Thoughts on Alcohol Use and Abuse

A little alcohol can boost creativity and strengthen
social ties. But there's nothing moderate, or convivial,
about the way many Americans drink today.
—Kate Julian, *The Atlantic*[1]

Drinking Habits Change Slowly

Though journalist Kate Julian's assessment of America's drinking problem seems quite sweeping, there is some truth to what she is saying. Old habits are hard to shake or brake, and Americans' drinking habits are changing only slowly. There are some positive developments, but also some rather worrisome ones, hearkening back to this country's "spectacular binge" habits.

The good news is that wine drinking is on the rise and with it a rather different drinking culture. It was introduced by European immigrants and Americans who experienced a more wholesome drinking culture in Europe and wanted to see such a culture grow here in the US. Robert Mondavi, the son of Italian immigrants, for example, not only helped develop a thriving wine industry in Napa Valley, California, but also created a carefully curated culture with it: wine enjoyed in the context of meals around the dinner table, concerts, festive celebrations, and communal gatherings not only for the enjoyment of wine but also for thoughtful conversation. I had the joy to interview his son Tim Mondavi for my book *The Spirituality of Wine*, and he even hosted me at his boutique winery for a talk on the spirituality of wine, and we explored wine tasting as a spiritual practice together.[2] I was impressed by the family's commitment not only to produce high-quality wine but also to encourage a more wholesome drinking culture.

Such initiatives are popping up all over the country and seem promising to me. I have visited wineries in California, Oregon, Washington, Virginia, Texas, and even Alabama, and the feel I get is similar to what I have grown up with: not binge drinking but a desire to learn about wine and how to embrace a balanced and moderate approach to enjoying alcohol. They do so by learning how to pair wine with food, observing how wine can enhance conversation, creativity, and conviviality, and learning through all of this how to grow a stronger sense of community and belonging. Increasingly, Americans find this an attractive way forward.

I first met my husband at a chapter dinner of the International Wine and Food Society (IWFS) in Birmingham, a society devoted to cultivating an atmosphere of enjoying wine and food together, seasoned with thoughtful conversation and convivial celebration. Having grown up on a winery where we did just that, I felt right at home and knew that this convivial group would help me settle into my new home. I made some precious friends at these gatherings, and I even found a lovely and charming husband there. Way to go, IWFS!

The bad news is that binge drinking is still prevalent, especially among college students and younger Americans. The National Center for Drug Abuse Statistics added a new category called "high-intensity drinking," a worrisome and highly dangerous practice. Americans on average drink twice as much distilled spirits as Western Europeans do, while Western Europeans drink more than twice as much wine as Americans do.

I have always felt uneasy about how much whiskey, bourbon, and potent cocktails Americans indulge in. It is here that the drinking habits of Americans diverge quite significantly from those of Western Europe, the culture I grew up in. It is not that distilled spirits are not present, but they play a much smaller role and there is a cultural awareness that distilled spirits are more dangerous than less potent beverages such as wine and beer. It is not culturally accepted that one indulges in distilled spirits on a regular basis. No one in my circle of friends in Germany goes home after a long day of work and pours a glass or two of whiskey or brandy to wind down and decompress.

On our family winery, we have a small distillery, and my dad made a range of distilled beverages, including brandy made from wine and schnapps made from our own fruit orchards (pear, plum, and apple), but these were high-quality spirits with incredible natural and subtle aromas and were served only sparingly. The government keeps a watchful eye on its operation, and we have to report minutely on when and for how long we operate it. Licenses are hard to come by and highly restrict how much a distiller can produce. They are precious drops of concentrated natural fruit aroma clothed in alcohol and kept for very special occasions.

We never drank distilled spirits regularly, and they were usually served at festive occasions at the end of a long meal as a digestive. Occasionally Dad made us drink a schnapps when we had an upset stomach. Neighboring countries such as Italy and France have similar drinking cultures: distilled spirits, whether cognac or grappa, are usually served sparingly as an aperitif or digestive in the context of a leisurely meal. It is worrisome to me that distilled spirits are still the second most preferred alcoholic beverage in America, and it speaks to me of a very different drinking culture, a culture that is only slowly changing.

Some Sobering Statistics

America came of age on distilled spirits and strong cider, and this profoundly shaped the way Americans still drink today. New drinking habits began to emerge after the American Prohibition in the 1950s. I think it is enlightening to look at some statistics to understand how the country is evolving. International statistics measure alcohol consumption in the form of pure alcohol content consumed in various forms per year per person in liters. In 1950 the average annual pure alcohol consumption in beer was approximately 2.752 liters, while distilled spirits was 2.043 liters. Wine consumption was only 0.418 liters back then. Over the last seventy years, alcohol consumption has fluctuated considerably and beer has remained the most popular drink. In the early 1980s it increased to more than four liters, and distilled spirits to more than three liters. Distilled spirits climaxed in the mid 1970s to 3.1 liters. These were heavy drinking days for Americans. Since then, there has been some ebb and flow, but a gradual decline in beer and distilled spirits consumption can be traced alongside a steady increase in wine consumption. By 2003 Americans on average drank 3.627 liters of beer, distilled spirits decreased to 2.011 liters, and wine increased to 1.001 liters. By 2018 Americans drank on average 3.245 liters of beer, distilled spirits increased to 2.600 liters, and wine increased to 1.211 liters of wine.[3]

Though alcohol consumption might be changing, the drinking patterns of Americans are still worrisome. Americans have one of the highest rates of alcohol- and drug-use disorders and addictions of various kinds. Alongside alcohol, drug, and gambling addictions, newer forms such as addictions to shopping, internet use and social media, gaming, pornography, and workaholism have ravaged through society.[4] Alcohol-related deaths have increased significantly over the last two decades.[5] The National Survey on Drug Use and Health of the USA from 2021 reports that approximately 47.5 percent of Americans ages twelve and older drank alcohol in the last thirty days (down from 51.1 percent in 2013 and 55.3 percent in 2018). In addition, 21.5 percent of Americans ages twelve and older have practiced binge drinking in the last thirty days (down by 1.5 percent from since 2013). The rate is higher among college students:[6] 5.8 percent reported heavy drinking (down from 6.5 percent in 2013).[7] The rate of alcohol dependence among adults declined slightly from 7.7 percent in 2002 to 6.7 percent in 2022.[8]

Americans consume comparable amounts of alcohol to residents of the United Kingdom, where alcohol consumption has decreased over the last decade among younger people.[9] Germany and France have a higher rate of alcohol consumption, but they drink less distilled spirits and most of the alcohol consumed is wine or beer, which is often enjoyed with food around the dinner table, an important part of European culture. The share of distilled spirits is nearly 35 percent in the USA and 9.8 percent in Italy, less than 19 percent in Germany, and just over 20 percent in France.[10]

The National Center for Drug Abuse Statistics' new category of "high-intensity drinking" is described as two to three times more alcohol consumed than under the "binge drinking" category (five or more drinks on the same occasion).[11] This is a frightening development, and it is the younger generation that is most prone to abuse alcohol this way.[12]

It is quite revealing that alcohol use and abuse statistics do not differentiate between the various forms of alcohol that are being consumed.[13] I think this is an oversight that needs to be corrected. It does matter whether one consumes a glass of bourbon at home or in a bar, or sips a glass of wine as part of a shared meal. The table culture that celebrates wine as part of a communal meal is very different from that of bars, where shots of whiskey and potent cocktails can lure you much more easily and quickly into a state of severe intoxication. Distilled spirits are a different animal, easily taking on beastly forms, clenching their fierce claws into the fragile fabric of American society.

Increasingly, Americans are drinking alone, whether in the home or at a bar, and this is a truly worrisome development. The film *Avalon* traces the decline of a large, multigenerational American immigrant family and with it the disappearance of mealtimes together around the table. The raw and heartwrenching ending of the film only foreshadows what would happen in the decades to come: for the first time in human history, many families do not eat together around the table anymore. It is truly shocking.[14] Eating and drinking are becoming increasingly solitary experiences in our society.[15] Sociological studies like Robert Putnam's *Bowling Alone* show that Americans are less and less engaged in social affairs and spend more and more time at home alone engaged in passive activities such as watching TV. This is only exacerbated by the internet and social media. We find ourselves in a barren social landscape, and it is tempting to reach for a glass of spirits to quench the deep ache within.

19

Some Sobering Stories on Alcohol Use and Abuse

I saw how easily, how swiftly, how imperceptibly
you could slip into a habit.
—Gabrille Glaser, *Her Best-Kept Secret*[1]

On a summer vacation at some resort in Mexico . . .
I swam up to the pool bar. It was eleven a.m., and I
ordered two shots of tequila and two Coronas.
—Holly Whitaker, *Quit Like a Woman*[2]

Contemporary Patterns Explored

It is not easy in America to develop a healthy and wholesome relationship with wine and alcohol more widely speaking. Whether it is in working environments, raising your children in affluent neighborhoods where children's parties turn into an excuse for parents to start drinking early, or sending your teenagers off to college, where binge drinking is often a part of the American college experience, unhealthy drinking patterns permeate large swaths of American society. They are not new. They are a subconscious return to old patterns fueled by the excessive marketing of the alcohol industry and the incredibly pressured and stressful lives we often live.[3]

Popular authors Holly Whitaker and Annie Grace, both recovering alcoholics, argue that the way forward is not to drink alcohol at all. They are part of a new temperance movement. The drinking culture they got caught up in had no boundaries, no questioning of unhealthy habits, no wisdom from parents passed down from their parents, just the impulse to drink and the need to conform to the stressful and demanding environments they inhabited. They have never experienced a culture in which drinking wine was done well.

I sometimes find myself in social settings where I am offered a glass of wine or a cocktail before 5:00 p.m., and I always decline, saying, "I don't drink before five o'clock!" The response I often get is quite telling: "It's five o'clock somewhere!" It's a tongue-in-cheek comment, but behind it lies a serious problem. There are no cultural boundaries in America for when it is okay to have a glass of wine or to drink alcohol. There is a lack of wisdom, a cultural void that fails to put in place the boundaries that we need as a society to develop a healthier relationship with alcohol.

It was when I began talking to my friends in Birmingham that I realized that I carry deep within me the wisdom not only of my parents and my grandparents but of a whole culture that learned over many centuries to drink wine wisely. The Romans brought vines to our region in Bavaria, but it was Benedictine nuns in the seventh century who planted vineyards along the hillsides that my family continues to cultivate more than 1,400 years later. Wine has been with us for a long time, and a cultural knowledge and wisdom emerged that helped create a sustainable wine-drinking culture.

These Benedictine nuns crafted wine for the Lord's Supper, and my family continues to do so for our Lutheran church. Studies have confirmed that those who are socialized into drinking alcohol in a religious context are less likely to abuse it.

Living in the American South, where many have grown up in families and churches where drinking alcohol is taboo, there aren't lots of cultural rules in place to guide individuals in their relationship with wine. Stories of alcohol abuse abound in their families: grandparents, parents, or siblings. The deep wound of the "spectacular binge" still lingers, and the polar opposites of abstinence and binge drinking still have a profound hold on Southern drinking culture, and perhaps the country as a whole.

Some Sobering Stories

My friend Trish is married, has two young children in school, and has been very successful in her career. Two of her stepsiblings are recovering alcoholics. She lives in an affluent neighborhood, and her life is hectic. In her late twenties, she discovered wine and loves learning about wine, terroir, and how to pair wine with food. She has a wonderful group of friends but realizes that all of their gatherings center around alcohol, mostly wine. She has experienced a wonderful wine culture when traveling in Europe, but this culture is hard to live by in her own community. Her normal pace of life is to always be pushed to the limits. It is like a torrent that she feels sucked into. And with it comes junk food and alcohol. It is a torrent that she finds hard to step out of. A lot of her mom friends are working mothers, and so they work hard and play hard, and this often includes alcohol. They had a mimosa party to celebrate that they got their children through kindergarten. When they go for brunch—and more and more restaurants are offering brunch now—they enjoy mimosas, champagne, seltzers, or Bloody Marys. Without blinking, Trish tells me that day drinking is a trend. When they throw children's parties, the parents start drinking hard seltzer and beer in the afternoon, in front of their children. I was shocked to hear this and felt I was living in my own little bubble only a few miles away. I called my niece in Germany, who is also a young mother, and asked whether such habits were common in her circles. I was relieved to hear that her generation continues to follow the habits of old and that coffee and tea and cake are served for adults at children's parties, and they drink wine only in the evening, if at all. Trish attends a conservative church, and I would have thought that meant having conservative drinking habits. I was mistaken.

My friend Lily is a heavy drinker, and sometimes I worry about her drinking habits. When her daughter graduated from high school, she invited me to the graduation. Lily's best friend from college and her sister joined us, and we all gathered at Lily's house to drive to the college campus. No alcohol is officially allowed there. Before we left, Lily emptied water bottles and filled them up with vodka to take to the graduation ceremony. I couldn't believe my eyes. Then they turned to me to ask whether I wanted one as well. I declined, trying to hide my surprise. Apparently, this is quite a common practice, and there are now various booze-hiding devices available to make smuggling hard liquor into events more cunning: flasks masquerading as sunscreen lotion, hair brushes, tampons, binoculars, and pocket umbrellas, even books containing not pages with words but flasks hidden between the covers. Secretive drinking seems to be on the rise again, and it does not help a society to develop a healthier relationship with alcohol.

A few years back, I went to the beach on the Gulf Coast of Alabama with a few friends, a major pastime for Southerners. I was looking forward to experiencing it. When we got ready in the morning and collected our towels, chairs, and sunscreen to go to the beach, my friend Charles pulled out a massive thermos bottle and began mixing Margaritas to take with us to the beach. I was stunned and wondered, Did he not know that drinking alcohol while sunbathing poses some real health risks? And why should we be drinking alcohol that early in the day anyway? It was one of those tense cultural moments when I felt disoriented and, yes, angry. I thought it was a dangerous habit, but for Charles it was a normal and natural thing to do: all his peers did it as well.

My friend George is in his seventies and is a recovering alcoholic. He has been sober for nearly twenty-three years. He started drinking in his late teens, but it was the business culture he worked in that set him on the path to alcoholism. Some of his worst drinking happened from the mid 1970s to the late 1990s, when Americans in general experienced a heavy drinking period. He worked in an industrial environment where factory workers drank heavily and so did the management. Drinking over a business lunch was normal, and sometimes he started the day off with a Bloody Mary for breakfast. He traveled all over the US and entertained business partners at night, making good use of his generous spending account, ordering really nice wines for his guests. George confessed that he never cared for the taste of wine, beer, and spirits. It was the feelings they gave him that made him drink to escape the reality of his inner turmoil. He carried a deep sense of shame within, and alcohol snapped him out of the feeling for a bit, but it never lasted. A tragic car accident woke him up, and he sought help with Alcoholics Anonymous.

My friend Anne is a single mother with two beautiful young teenage daughters. She is constantly worried about her girls because high schoolers' drinking habits are difficult to control. Secret drinking parties in the basements of unassuming parents are a normal event on the weekends. Her daughter Lee tells me that almost everyone at her high school has a fake ID by their final year and all kids drink. The boys drink more straight liquor, while the girls drink seltzers. Lee says that there is incredible peer pressure to drink and to believe that the best fun is only to be had when drinking.

These are sobering stories and should give us pause. I do not espouse the idea that all of us should stop drinking because some abuse it. I think this is not only unrealistic but also unbiblical. The unhealthy should not determine the lives of the healthy, but we should be aware of the dangers of alcohol even as we explore wine's blessed benefits. Both Martin Luther and John Calvin insisted we must not forbid the drinking of wine or withhold the enjoyment of wine and therefore God's kindness toward us. Calvin called this kind of thinking an "inhuman philosophy."[4] Some need not drink. For the rest of us, the challenge remains to develop a healthy and wholesome relationship with wine. This is a task not only for individuals but also, perhaps more important, for society at large. The church has a crucial role to play here: wine as a gift from God has a special mission, and only the church understands what this mission is and can help bring it to fruition.

PART 5

SAVORING OURSELVES INTO WONDER WITH WINE

20

Lady Wisdom
Plants a Vineyard

*No nation is . . . sober, where the dearness of wine
substitutes ardent spirits as the common beverage. It is,
in truth, the only antidote to the bane of whiskey.*
—Thomas Jefferson, former president of
the United States of America[1]

*[A wise woman] considers a field and buys it; with the
fruit of her hands she plants a vineyard.*
—Proverbs 31:16

Cultivating Wisdom Together

Thomas Jefferson gained much wisdom while living in France at the
dawn of the French Revolution. He observed that the French were
not given to excessive drinking as they lived through tumultuous
times. This is probably what made Jefferson believe that wine was

the antidote to the bane of whiskey. It is unrealistic to think that whiskey will ever be banned in the United States: its cultural and economic hold is too strong. However, what can and hopefully will happen is that wine will continue to become more popular and eventually overtake spirits as the second most consumed alcoholic beverage in America.

The French had learned from the Benedictines and Cistercians that wine is a gift from God, and over many centuries they were socialized into drinking wine through the religious ritual of the Eucharist, church-related feasts, and the widespread traditions of culture: families enjoying wine together with food around the dinner table where children were able to observe their parents and grandparents closely and emulate them. It was a much slower and more communal process of drinking than we often experience today in our fast-paced societies, where solitary drinking has become so popular and a quick drink at a bar the prelude or postlude to an evening out.

Cultures do change over time and with new generations. It is time that we take a step back and ask how we can cultivate a more wholesome relationship with wine not just as individuals but as a society, and within this society as a decidedly Christian community. We can and must shake old cultural habits and embrace new ones. The church has not helped us develop a better understanding of wine and how to enjoy it because alcohol has been such a taboo subject and pastors and priests have been wary to address it. This can change. We can reclaim wine as a gift from God and learn how to enjoy it. It means engaging in an open and honest conversation about it and purposefully implementing new ways of consuming wine, allowing our most precious sacrament of the Lord's Supper to speak to us in new ways.

I do believe that we need to move away from drinking so much hard liquor and rediscover wine as gift from God that we can enjoy in the context of meals shared around the dinner table. Our times and cultures are vastly different than those of the Bible. As we ponder how we can learn from the Bible to enjoy wine as a gift from God, we can also rediscover a more communal life around the table, sharing meals as a spiritual and cultural practice, and develop a slower and more contemplative life.

Wine is not an isolated consumer product advertised in the Bible. It is embedded in God's revealed story of creation and redemption that sees Jesus and the Spirit at work in all things, including the enjoyment of a glass of well-crafted wine. The Bible calls us to live redemptively and wisely in God's presence, so it is time that we allowed the Bible to infuse our personal and communal drinking habits with divine wisdom.

Lady Wisdom Plants a Vineyard and Serves Wine

What I would like to do here is offer some reflections, inspired by my research on wine in the Bible and my own cultural understanding. You may agree or disagree with me, but I hope that you can take away some points of reflection and ponder them. I believe we can and should have a wider conversation in our churches that will help us embrace a more healing and wholesome relationship with wine and alcohol.

I believe the church needs to reclaim wine's important place in the celebration of the Lord's Supper. Before the Reformation, all churches had the following important prayer included as part of their liturgy, drawing on the Jewish roots of the Passover liturgy: "Blessed are you, Lord God of all creation, for through your goodness we have received the wine we offer you: fruit of the vine and work of human hands, it will become our spiritual drink."

Christians heard this prayer at least once a week. This prayer draws us into a cosmic vision where wine and viticulture are not secular matter but imbued with spiritual meaning.[2] It instills in us a profound understanding of wine as a gift from God that we are to receive with gratitude and joy. And this prayer points to and celebrates the beautiful divine-human collaboration that is at work when wine is thoughtfully crafted. The beauty we find in well-crafted wine should lift our hearts in awe to God, our benevolent creator, and make us grateful for all who are involved in the hard work of agriculture.

My church occasionally includes this prayer for special services, such as Earth Sunday, but not as the permanent fixture of the liturgy it used to be. Perhaps the latent ambivalence toward wine and alcohol continues to haunt us as a church. How are Christians to learn that bread and wine, food and agriculture are not secular things, devoid of spiritual meaning, but gifts from God? Only when we see them as spiritual gifts can we understand that God wants to heal our relationship with both wine and food.

Increasingly, even Episcopalians and Anglicans dip the wafer into the chalice rather than taking a good sip of wine from the one chalice, symbolizing our unity as Christians. The pandemic has made us wary of too much physical contact, but we are missing out on a powerful sensory experience that helps us ingest the profoundest spiritual realities. Has not Christ invited us to take this cup and drink from it? Did God not imbue us with the gifts of touch, smell, and taste so we could know him better? When I walk away from the Lord's Supper and feel the wine on my tongue and as it glides down my throat, I feel the warmth of God's presence in my body and not just as an idea in my head.

We can also celebrate with wine important religious feasts such as Easter, Pentecost, and Christmas, as well as baptisms, confirmations, and weddings, and model to our children and grandchildren a way of enjoying wine as part of our spirituality that honors God and his gifts to us. Scientific studies have shown that children who are socialized into drinking wine in religious settings are less likely to abuse it later in life. Jewish communities, for example, teach their children that wine is a sacred gift, that drinking it is an act of communion, and that drunkenness is a profanity.[3] We all can help to model a wholesome way of enjoying wine.

The Bible invites us to enjoy wine in the community of the saints, not as lone rangers or in the secrecy of our homes. God's gift of wine calls us into the community that is the body of Christ. It is here that we learn to live the Christian life and what it means to love God and our neighbor. We heal in community and not apart from it. If you feel stressed and anxious, don't reach for a bottle. Call a friend or reach out to someone in your church. I encourage you not to get into the habit of drinking by yourself, or if you have already established this habit, to try to wean yourself of it. Join a group that enjoys wine and experience how wine savored in community has the benefit of helping you feel more connected in a playful and relaxed way. Conviviality is a powerful antidote to loneliness and the isolation that many of us feel, even when we are among people.

Jesus and the Jewish community he lived in drank wine in the contexts of communal meals: the Passover meal, Sabbath celebrations, wedding feasts, and of course regular family meals. Make it a habit to drink wine mostly with a meal or at least some finger food, such as charcuterie or cheese. It will provide a framework for and limits to when you will drink wine. That way it will become something special rather than something you use habitually to help you wind down after work or nurse an anxious spirit. It is easy to disengage from our more difficult emotions and distract ourselves in ways that won't nourish our spirits and help us heal. When I am stressed or worn down, I try to go out into my garden to find a quiet presence that helps me unwind and feel what I need to feel. Sometimes I do gentle stretching exercises to feel where my stress manifests in the body, and I try to listen to it, hold it gently, and find release through kind attention to myself. Tend to your soul. Reserve your glass of wine for when you are with others to enjoy wine, food, and conversations that enrich your soul.

We live in a consumer society where marketing machines surround us constantly, offering us beverages they tell us will make us feel happy, cool, hip, and with it. It is hard not to be entangled in this web of advertising and the consumer culture it creates. We live in a cultural moment when consumerism is a kind of spirituality that helps us define who we are and to whom we belong depending on what we consume: whether that is the neighborhoods we live in, the cars we drive, the holidays we can afford, the clothes we wear, or the kind of alcohol we drink.[4] In theory we know that as Christians our worth and our identity are not defined by the brands we consume, but once we step out of the church and scroll through our phones and compare ourselves with others, it isn't easy to disentangle ourselves from it all.

The wine we drink in the celebration of the Lord's Supper beckons us to a new way of consuming: we don't need to secure for ourselves a place in this world anymore. Christ has set us free to live as God's beloved children. We can and must learn to see wine, and for that matter all we consume, as a gift from God that he gave so we can commune more deeply with him and with each other and honor those who produce it.[5] We consume to commune, and we must learn not to be enslaved by the things we consume.

Wisdom Builds a House

A new era is dawning. Vineyards are being planted all over North America and every state in the US now has a winery.[6] This is not a secular matter. We must reclaim wine as a gift from God. Former pastors find themselves pouring wine in the hospitality industry as their new vocation.[7] Thomas Jefferson would be relieved to hear this, and now we need to learn how to consume wine wisely. It is time to build a new house inspired by the great architect of human flourishing.

In the German wine culture I grew up in, we do not usually drink before 5:00 p.m., except perhaps on a Sunday with our Sunday roast. We also don't drink wine every day. It is good to take a break and reserve wine for special gatherings. People in Europe tend to sit together for longer periods of time. Wine drinking is spread out over a long evening, sharing food and stories, allowing conviviality to gather momentum. Perhaps we can learn not to rush off too quickly but linger with each other and with the wine we enjoy. Mindfulness is a wonderful movement in our contemporary society, and perhaps applying mindfulness to our enjoyment of wine is a good way to connect savoring wine with a spiritual discipline.

It is quite common in the United States to involve alcohol in business meetings and work-related gatherings. Consider not drinking alcohol in these contexts, or drinking very little. It is wise to stay alert and sober in professional contexts. In your personal life, it might be helpful to think through how you would like to enjoy wine. If you are married, you can discuss with your spouse certain rhythms and boundaries you would like to establish in your family. If you are single or live alone, invite some close friends to help you think through what relationship you would like to have with wine. Drink wine wisely as you welcome others to your table and savor the goodness of God in a glass of well-crafted wine.

> Wisdom has built her house; she has hewn her seven pillars. . . . [S]he has mixed her wine; she has also set her table.
>
> —Proverbs 9:1–2

Wine to Gladden
the Human Heart

You . . . bring forth food from the earth and
wine to gladden the human heart.
—Psalm 104:14–15

Consuming Redemptively?

As I look back on my interviews with a wide range of Christians on their use of alcohol, I think of my friend's daughter Lee, who shared about the drinking habits of high schoolers in the heart of the Bible Belt here in Birmingham, Alabama. She shared with me about her peers' desperate attempts, fueled by significant peer pressure, to have fun with alcohol, mostly vodka and strong seltzers. Many of the Christian professionals I interviewed disclosed that "work hard, play hard" is the mantra that defines the rhythm of their daily lives like a secular liturgy. It justifies their desire to compensate for their strong work ethic and exhausting work day with an equally strong urge to have fun and consume liberally, including generous amounts of often cheap alcohol. Heavy drinking is the pendulum swing of a younger Christian generation that, having been raised by abstinent parents and grandparents, feels finally free to have some "fun."

These conversations reminded me of a book I read in graduate school by Neil Postman, poignantly called *Amusing Ourselves to Death*. In it he explores how a culture can become addicted to amusement and fun, and Postman sees this as a kind of oppression. He rightly fears that our obsession with entertainment and amusement will erode politics and public discourse, and it surely has. Neil Postman's writing has a prophetic tone, and with the advent of social media our addiction to entertainment, amusement, and consumerism has only gotten worse. Before we are anything else, it seems, we are consumers in the never-ending pursuit of getting and spending, eroding our spiritual prowess.[1] In a culture where our lives are so entangled with entertainment and consumerism as alternative spiritualities that tug and pull our hearts relentlessly, how are we to rediscover a Christian understanding of joy? And what role does wine have in eliciting this sense of joy? As advertising companies design their tunes to pull the strings of our desires toward the brands they want us to consume, how can we learn to consume redemptively?

> When a population becomes distracted by trivia, when cultural life is redefined as a perpetual round of entertainments, when serious public conversation becomes a form of baby-talk, when, in short, a people become an audience and their public business a vaudeville act, then a nation finds itself at risk; a culture-death is a clear possibility.
>
> —Neil Postman, *Amusing Ourselves to Death*

Wine to Gladden
the Human Heart

It is beautiful how Psalm 104 helps us do that, to consume redemptively. The psalmist here hearkens back to the creation account and the garden of Eden, literally meaning the garden of pleasure and delight. In Eden humans lived in harmonious communion with God and each other, enjoying the bounty of all that God gave them. This harmonious communion broke down with the fall. The psalmist firmly believes in God's redemption and invites us to reimagine this place and see ourselves in it, not as consumers but as recipients of God's gifts in food and wine, with our souls turned toward him in awe, wonder, and gratitude: "Bless the LORD, O my soul. O LORD my God, you are very great. You are clothed with honor and majesty" (Ps. 104:1).

The whole world is presented to us in the Bible as one all-embracing banqueting table.[2] In this biblical vision, farmers and vintners are agrarian priests who till the sacred soil, where heaven and earth mingle into fruitfulness. The psalmist points to God as the ultimate creator and grower of our food: "You cause the grass to grow for the cattle and plants for people to cultivate, to bring forth food from the earth and wine to gladden the human heart" (vv. 14–15). All that the earth brings forth is meant for communion with God, who in his love and benevolence provides for us in great abundance: "These all look to you to give them their food in due season; when you give to them, they gather it up; when you open your hand, they are filled with good things" (vv. 27–28). The psalmist invites us to envision God opening his hand and seeing it filled with the bounty of creation that he offers to us as a gift. It speaks of an incredible presence. God is with us and provides so generously for us. This is the reason for our joy.

Rather than allowing ourselves to be constantly bombarded by marketing machines with images of the brands—mostly of highly processed foods and drinks—that they want us to consume, the psalmist invites us to take a step back. Today, praying this psalm beckons us to disentangle ourselves from social media, turn off the TV, and pay attention to the natural world. Step outside for a moment and realize that all you see, the heavens and the earth, the clouds and the winds, fire and flames, oceans and mountains, springs and valleys, are where God's glory is revealed.

All that the earth brings forth, including bread and wine and oil, are bountiful gifts we receive from God's hand. The psalmist wants to reorient our lives from being obedient consumers to becoming attentive and grateful recipients of God's gifts, including the special gift of wine. Joy arises out of this revelatory awareness of who God is and what he desires to give to us so benevolently. And a well-crafted wine has the added benefit of helping to elicit this joy in us with its alcohol clothed in delicious beauty that stirs our senses and our souls toward gratitude and joy. Sure, you can drink wine to get a little buzz, have some fun, and not think of God at all. You might not even care whether the wine has any particular taste, and you might drink it purely for the little lift it can give you.

The Bible, however, invites us to savor wine as a gift from God that will make us giddy in body and spirit. We are loved. The earth, as God's handmaiden, provides for us. These blissful moments of savoring wine were always meant to stir our souls toward wonder and awe and joy as we welcome God's presence in our midst. We can learn to be more purposeful about how we consume wine and allow a convivial spirit to nurture our relationships, strengthen bonds of kinship and friendship, deepen our conversations, and inspire our creative collaborations.

As part of my work around reclaiming wine as a gift from God, I have been holding wine tastings as a spiritual practice. The purpose of these evenings is to help our guests experience what it can look like to understand and receive wine as a gift from God, allow a wine tasting to help us relax and open up to God's presence, to the gift of joy, to each other, and forge deeper bonds. It takes a certain atmosphere for many of us to feel comfortable to allow our conversations to move from superficial banter to more vulnerable and honest conversations. Here redemptive exchanges of feelings and thoughts can happen where we can hold each other gently in the sacred space of communal bonding. In appendix 1, I provide instructions for how to do a wine tasting as a spiritual practice so you can learn to facilitate this way of receiving wine as a gift from God.

Consuming Redemptively and with Great Joy

We live in a culture where consumerism as a kind of spirituality has become deeply entrenched, and often we are not even aware of how it shapes us. We need to find new ways of consuming that free us up to welcome the Spirit's redemptive work in our midst and bring us to where a deep sense of joy is the bright star that leads us home to the celestial city.

The Lord's Supper teaches us that wine has become a sanctified vehicle of God's judgment, forgiveness, and healing in our world. Our lives are not without purpose or destiny. In Christ, our lives are now oriented toward God's redemptive presence. We are called to be part of this movement where the Holy Spirit woos us constantly to receive forgiveness and welcome healing and share it with this broken world.

The battle we fight is against a kind of consumerism that does not want us to heal. Neil Postman was right. We find ourselves in an oppressive matrix that seeks to hollow out our spiritual lives. Marketing strategies capitalize on our most vulnerable and weak parts and attack the pleasure centers of our brains. They want to make us consume rather than heal, because if we were to heal and be free, we would not need their brands to make us feel good or worthy or to give us a sense of belonging. Brands will not heal us. If we use them to make us feel better, then they are like fire poured on our festering inner wounds. The gospel is meant to set us free of all of this, but does it?

We can embrace God's forgiveness and healing by learning to consume redemptively. Don't drink wine or alcohol to disengage from the hard stuff of life. Don't drown your sorrows in alcohol. Don't give in to the anxious desire to belong to a crowd given to heavy drinking as a way to be entertained and find meaningful experiences of joy. You won't find it there. Don't lick your wounds by buying yet another outfit or another electronic gadget or by mixing yet another cocktail. Don't run away from the pain you carry within.

Next time you go up to the altar to receive the cup, take a deep sip and feel with your tongue and throat and your whole body Christ's blood shed for you so you can be free. Wine creates powerful sensations in the body. Listen to these sensations as the spiritual messengers they were always meant to be. There is a reason why Jesus chose wine. It is a powerful and potent way to bring a message across. Allow God to speak to you through the wine. Pause for a moment and tell God that you are willing to embrace the journey of healing. Do not be afraid to gaze into the abyss that you might find within. God is right there with you to lead you through your valley of tears into the freedom that God's love and grace offer you.

My friend George had gone to church most of his life. He carried within him a deep sense of shame, and the voice of shame became like a familiar friend, always there to make him feel worthless. It was a vicious cycle. It took a scary accident to wake him up and make him seek help. He had heard sermon upon sermon, received the Lord's Supper, and been surrounded by Christians all of his life, and yet he was stuck.

Becoming unstuck is our great challenge so we can begin and continue the journey of healing that all Christians are called upon to make. Consuming the bread and wine in the Lord's Supper calls us to experience God's forgiveness and healing. You have to ingest salvation and make it your own. Drinking wine from the eucharistic cup means swallowing the wine and ingesting it, allowing it to become part of your innermost life and being transformed by it.

The journey of healing is often painful. We have to return to sore wounds to allow them to heal. Just like grapes are crushed so that the juice can be pressed out and flow freely and be fermented into wine, so do we need to allow Christ to peel away our defenses so that our souls are free to heal and join the great spiritual community of the body of Christ. As this spiritual community, we are called to inhabit an atmosphere of love, forgiveness, and acceptance where the healing power of the Spirit can move freely. As we participate in the Lord's Supper, we are free to consume in order to commune, and joy comes to us as a gift. It is here that wine can help elicit this sense of joy, for God gave wine to make glad our hearts and help us sing the song of salvation.

22

On Earth as It Is in Heaven

Feasting in God's Kingdom

On this mountain the LORD *of hosts will make for all peoples
a feast of rich food, a feast of well-aged wines, of rich food
filled with marrow, of well-aged wines strained clear.*
—Isaiah 25:6

*"Quickly . . . get the fatted calf and kill it, and let
us eat and celebrate, for this son of mine was dead
and is alive again; he was lost and is found!"*
—Luke 15:22–24

The Allure of Our Surroundings

The other day my husband and I went to a supermarket in an affluent part of town. We do not often go there, but it was on our way
home from a gathering with friends, and so we stopped to pick up
some groceries. A massive sign was right in front of the only entrance
to the supermarket: "GOT A LIST? GET A DRINK. You can now
enjoy beer or wine while you shop."

Then in very small print at the lower left, hardly readable, it
said, "Drink responsibly. Be 21." I had a strong emotional response
to it, and it was not a positive one. This advertisement is a great
example of the mixed messages we get in our society about drinking. There are no boundaries anymore; you can now drink at any
time, and supermarkets make it culturally acceptable and even
fashionable. Even such mundane tasks as shopping for groceries is
no longer a hindrance to imbibing a little alcohol. I won't even mention that it encourages drinking and driving, for most people drive
to the supermarket.

The sign is also a great example of how the marketing world
capitalizes on alcohol to make it serve their agenda. The marketing experts know that a little alcohol will give us an emotional
lift, help us relax, let our cognitive defenses down, and be a little
more liberal with our money. It's the perfect tool for luring us into
spending more and buying things we don't intend to buy. They
don't say that out loud, of course; they just find a pithy slogan to
lure us in.

In the swamplands of manipulative marketing, the prayers
of the Psalter regarding our enemies have new and urgent meaning: "They flush me out; now they surround me; they set their
eyes to cast me to the ground. They are like a lion eager to tear,
like a young lion lurking in ambush" (Ps. 17:11–12; see also
Ps. 22:12–13). The marketing experts know where to find us: in
the supermarkets, when we open our computers and look things
up on the internet, on social-media platforms like Instagram or
Facebook. They don't kill us outright. They just cast a shroud on
all people as they lure us in, help us bond with their brands, spend

a little too much money, and firmly establish us in the enslavement to things. We are all vulnerable to it because we are surrounded by it all the time.

On Earth as It Is in Heaven

Once a year I teach a class on the spirituality of food that includes a session about feasting as a spiritual practice. I like to use the parable of the Prodigal Son (Luke 15), which I call the parable of redemptive feasting. It is a wonderful example of how Jesus teaches us to feast: to celebrate our redemption, our homecoming, and God's unconditional love for us. God's love and grace extend to a place many of us would recoil from like the older son in the parable. He resents the Father's generosity in throwing a lavish feast for what he considers an unworthy and wayward brother. It's okay to welcome someone back into the fold, but throw a lavish feast and waste money on an undeserving vagabond?

When I tried to find some images that illustrate this feast in the history of Western art, I was quite surprised to find only artwork that depicts the dissolute living of the lost son or the loving embrace between father and son. I could not find one artist who thought it worthwhile to depict and explore this lavish feast in art. I think this is quite telling about how difficult it is for us to understand and imagine the role of feasting in our spiritual communities. We still have lingering ambivalent feelings about feasting when it comes to our spiritual lives. Parties? Oh, yes, please! But feasting as a way to nurture our spiritual lives?

Our churches and institutions of theological education, for the most part, do not teach us about feasting as a spiritual practice, about how wine can enhance our festive play before God. Many churches host AA meetings to support those who struggle with addictions to alcohol. I understand this because the church is called to offer God's healing to a broken world. And yet as Christians we are called to worship and celebrate the incredible gift of God's redeeming presence in our midst, and not just at short intervals around Christmas and Easter. As our societies are getting more secular, perhaps we need to expand our feasts not just around Christmas and Easter but also around Epiphany, Ascension, Pentecost, and ordinary Sundays and birthdays.

So where do we find those celebratory occasions, and where do we learn how to enjoy wine in redemptive ways? How do we celebrate and savor wine so that it deepens our sense of gratitude, enhances our joy, helps us open up to one another, inspires our conversations, and nurtures collaborative friendships for the sake of the kingdom of God? Does the Lord's Supper not invite us to believe that God wants to redeem all aspects of our lives, including our relationship with food and wine and how we feast? In the Bible, feasts and celebrations are important ways believers cultivate their spiritual lives and nurture spiritual communities. Jesus was even accused of being a glutton and drunkard because he attended so many dinner parties with all the wrong people. Food and wine were always meant to help us commune with God and bring heaven down to earth.

In my previous work, I examined the film *Babette's Feast* as a wonderful example of redemptive feasting. It is a profoundly moving film, and the unfolding of the lavish feast enhanced by choice selections of wines is wonderful to watch. Here the spiritual powers of food and wine are beautifully visualized as grace moves through gently intoxicated hearts and minds, melting away fear, bitterness, and resentment and releases a spirit of forgiveness and benevolence.[1]

And yet in our busy lives with limited resources, most of our feasting happens on a much smaller scale, and it takes creative collaboration to turn a gathering of friends into a spiritual feast. As we learn how to feast again, it can become a powerful witness to the world that we are a people set free to worship God and called to enjoy him forever. In our feasts great and small, heaven comes down to earth and lifts us up in a spirit of celebration and communion. We just have to relearn how to do it in ways that are both manageable for us and healing for our lives and communities. It is a spiritual and cultural treasure many of us have lost, and it is time to find it again.

Feasting in God's Kingdom

April is a busy month for us. We always invite a wide range of family and friends to celebrate Easter with us. It is a lot of work, and I try to have others bring something to share. My husband and I both work, and we are often tired and worn out by the time the weekend comes around. After Easter, as the end of the semester approaches, I prepare a feast for my students in our home because I want them to experience what feasting can be like. My friends Lois and Van from church always bring a salad from their organic garden, and my friend Janet makes a delicious dessert. It takes a big burden off my shoulders. Together with my husband, my friends turn into professional servers while I get to converse with my students and learn a little more about their lives and what the future might hold for them. The students, also worn out from a busy semester, get to pause for an evening and enjoy the feast. It is always a wonderful occasion, but it is a big commitment and sometimes I feel overwhelmed by it.

When I first began teaching at a seminary, my spiritual director and friend Eugene Peterson and his wife, Jan, came to visit me to help me settle in and encourage me in my work. Eugene impressed upon me that whatever the pressures are in teaching and writing, not to forget to practice hospitality. He encouraged me to be creative and ask others, including my students, to help make it happen. Eugene rarely told me what to do, and when he did, I listened carefully. I was already predisposed to practice hospitality because it was so deeply ingrained in my growing-up years on a family-run winery, but when life is busy and you feel worn down, it is tempting to let it slip. There are not many people who encourage me to keep doing it, but hospitality has always been fundamental to the life of the church, and it is a fairly recent development that it is not a common practice anymore. We need a renewed vision to see that hospitality and feasting are powerful ways to be the body of Christ and witness to the life that God has given us to share with the world.

My birthday is after Easter and after the end of the semester. I am usually tired and worn out by that time. Traditionally and culturally, we throw our own birthday parties in Germany and celebrate with family and friends. It is a communal celebration because we belong to our communities, and birthdays are an important time to pause and give thanks for the gift of life within that community. As adults, when life gets busy, it is easy to let go of it. Last year I was too tired, and my husband and I went out to eat for my birthday. It was nice, but something was lost: the feast and with it the sense of community and the joyous spirit that always hovers over it.

This year I decided not to let it slip again. I remembered Eugene's words and wrote to all my friends and asked them to bring something to share. Instead of gifts, I wrote, bring a salad or a bottle of wine. I thought of the people I wanted to invite: family and friends and some new friends that God had brought into our lives. I wanted it to be a time when we gather our community and reconnect and celebrate not just my birthday but the life that we share together. I felt grateful and wanted to express my gratitude. And we kept it simple: I made a Bavarian potato salad and we ordered sausages from our regenerative farmer, whose pigs forage forests and enjoy a rather blissful existence in the Black Belt of Alabama. As guests poured in and we offered up our small loaves and fishes, the table began to swell with a great bounty of food and wine.

Feasts were always meant to be like cathedrals in space and time that allow us to pause and celebrate the sacredness of all things: the gift of our lives embedded in communities of love, forgiveness, and care; our bodies that feast on food and wine as spiritual gifts; our homes as places of gathering, communing, and sharing. Christian feasting, at its best, gathers up the past, present, and future as we await the redemption of all things and welcome the Spirit's work in our midst.

We try to keep our wine refrigerator stocked with some lovely wines. It is an investment in God's future, for we know that the Lord of hosts likes to throw a party and be the host of a feast for all people, a feast of rich food, a feast of well-aged wine, where God's sacrificial love revealed in Jesus Christ welcomes us all home.

Savoring Ourselves into Wonder

"You have kept the good wine until now." Jesus did this,
the first of his signs, in Cana of Galilee and revealed
his glory, and his disciples believed in him.
—John 2:10–11

Ambivalent Feelings Linger

Most of us don't get to enjoy a good gulp of wine as we celebrate the Lord's Supper. It seems safer and more practical just to dip the wafer into the wine and skip a sensory experience that we don't understand anyway. In most of our Sunday school classes, we are no longer taught how to enjoy communion with God as we sip from the eucharistic cup, how to understand the meaning of wine in the cup, how to smell the wine, how to pay attention to the sensations as wine teases the bountiful taste buds on our tongues, as our noses smell its bouquet, and as the wine glides down our throats and warms our bodies. The early church, on the other hand, took great pains to help Christians understand this experience. It was important to them.[1]

Perhaps this is indicative of the lingering ambivalent feelings we have toward wine and food as spiritual gifts. Many of us experience food and wine as a battleground. Some fight a lonesome and hidden battle against the impulse of overeating, interspersed with seasons of restraint, on the desert island of their deepest longings. Others do not know and were never taught that food and wine are spiritual gifts meant to enrich our spiritual lives. And many have developed allergies and negative reactions to foods and wines because of how they are produced and the poor quality they come in. Many suffer from a range of diseases that are related to our unhealthy Western diet. Our relationship with food and wine is fraught with tensions and challenges. There are reasons for it.

One of them, I believe, is the long-held belief in the gluttony-temperance paradigm, first embraced by the Christian desert fathers. This paradigm has pushed us into believing that food and wine are battlegrounds.[2] John Cassian, who gathered up the wisdom of the desert fathers, warned us that the pleasure of eating is dangerous. As committed followers of Jesus, we must fight gluttony. Cassian encouraged his fellow desert fathers and mothers to fight overindulgence with temperance and restraint. In this spiritual vision, we try to take charge of our desires and urges and control our impulses. The emphasis lies on us and what we must do to get ahead of the game. We work hard at trying to control our actions, thoughts, and feelings so we don't eat and drink too much. These profound battles, experienced by so many Christians, have helped perpetuate our deep-seated ambivalence toward the senses of touch, taste, and smell for enriching our spiritual lives.

This ambivalence toward enjoying food and wine and our senses of smell and taste helped create an industry and food culture where the actual flavor of the basic ingredients is not important anymore. Buy a tomato or strawberries in the supermarket and tell me what you smell and taste: not much. Cheap mass-produced ingredients are processed into the foods we pick up at the supermarket, and plenty of sugar, salt, and fat are added to make sure they have flavor.

These monochrome flavors constantly scream at our taste buds and olfactory receptor cells, fueling our addictions to strong sensations.

> In a biblical interpretation of the virtue and vices paradigm, the opposite of the sin of gluttony is not the virtue of temperance, it is the virtue of savoring.
>
> —Gisela Kreglinger, *The Spirituality of Wine*

They have made us numb toward subtler and more delicate experiences. The more nuanced and beautiful tastes and smells of food and wine grown in vibrant and thriving soils are long forgotten. We don't even look for them anymore. They are like treasures lost in the engine of industrial agriculture. This forgotten treasure is as much a spiritual one as it is a cultural and agricultural one. God often speaks to us in the quiet whispers and wafts of gentle prodding, and we must learn once more what it means to be attentive to the great bounty of subtle renderings.

The good news is that food and wine were always intended for enjoyment and communion. Sadly, these wonderful tidings got buried in the history of Western Christianity as it developed ambivalent attitudes toward our senses of touch, taste, and smell. Our deepest hunger and thirst are always for God, and one way God invites us to commune with him is through the delicious food and wine we savor. They were always meant to be an invitation and instill within us a sense of wonder and awe for our Creator God.

Reclaiming Flavor, Reclaiming Wonder

Where do we turn to find the flavorful foods and wines that help us cultivate this sense of wonder and awe for what God has made? And where do the rich, subtle, and vibrant flavors come from anyway? These natural flavors of our foods and wines come from vibrant and

healthy soils and plants cultivated to bear fragrant fruit. All of this is
hard to come by these days. Our soils are leached of life and health,
and the plants grown are often winnowed out to produce quantity
over quality, visual perfection over rich flavors, shelf life over nourishing nutrients. Many Americans are overweight and at the same
time malnourished because readily available food and drink is high
in calories and low in nutrition. It is a world in desperate need of
God's redemption.

It was a secular movement that first forged the path to recover
the art of savoring for the life of the world. It emerged in Italy after
McDonald's had the audacity to open a fast-food restaurant right
by the Spanish steps in Rome. Italians have always prided themselves in being good stewards of a vibrant and sustainable food
and wine culture, but the fast-food movement did not come to a
grinding halt there.

Carlo Petrini, founder of the Slow Food movement, has worked
steadily with a celebratory spirit to preserve and reclaim the flavors
of the world.[3] Drawing on the image of Noah's ark, the Slow Food
movement works hard to protect and celebrate endangered heritage
foods and wines that are unique in taste, flavorful, and part of a dis-
tinct ecoregion. They call it the ark of taste. The manifold flavors
of the world and our experience of their smells, textures, and tastes
are not just cultural treasures, they are spiritual ones. They give us
a glimpse into the incredible splendor and beauty of this world and
instill in us a sense of wonder and awe for God, who made this world
so beautiful. The Slow Food movement now has chapters all over the
world, including the US. The Farm to Table movement was inspired
by it. In Birmingham, tucked away deep in the American South, we
have several restaurants, urban farms, and vibrant farmer's markets
all inspired in some way or another by the Slow Food movement.[4]

I have written earlier about our farmers and vintners as agrarian
priests. For too long we have abandoned the hard work of agriculture
and viticulture to corporate companies who do not care for revealing
the bounty God has placed into creation and are not interested in providing food that nourishes and heals our bodies. Their main goal is
profit. Our main goal is worship. Jesus compared the kingdom of God

to a treasure hidden in a field, and in the fields and hills are grown the treasures of food and wine that help us worship God, who imbued this earth with so much potential for beauty and nourishment.

As we search for vibrant beauty in food and wine, we must turn to and support those farmers and vintners who practice agriculture redemptively: healing the soil and producing foods that nourish our bodies and reveal this sense of beauty in the subtle and rich flavors of ripe fruit harvested in season. If you would like to search for a well-crafted wine that has expression and beauty to lift your heart heavenward, I do not recommend you go to Aldi or Trader Joe's. You will find cheap wines for sure, and their alcohol content will give you a little lift. But if you are looking for beautiful, fragrant, and vibrant wines, subtle and steady in their ability to move our senses toward wonder, amazement, and perhaps even awe, you must search for them like hidden treasures.[5]

Some object to this and argue that these foods and wines are more expensive and only affordable for the well-to-do. It is true, they are more expensive. They are costly in production and consumption. We must work together to make sure nourishing and delicious foods and wines are accessible to those who cannot afford them. New initiatives are being born that want to do just this. Perhaps it is not surprising that many of them happen outside the church rather than inside them. Jones Valley Teaching Farm in Birmingham, for example, has this prophetic vision, and they steadily work toward it. Not only do they grow fantastic fresh produce for the poor, they also teach students in poorer neighborhoods how to grow food and prepare it in delicious and nutritious ways.[6] Double Up Food Bucks also enables those in need to purchase more locally grown vegetables and fruits.[7] Food justice cannot be realized through cheap and unhealthy foods that makes the poor sick and ultimately poorer.[8] God's kingdom is more lavish than this. The prophet Isaiah's vision that God will make a feast of rich food with well-aged wine is not a metaphor for an otherworldly reality. It is an invitation to us Christians to bring heaven down to earth as we gather and feast together and share God's bounty with one another, especially with those who cannot afford it.

For many of us the question of cost is a question of priority. We just do not want to invest our money in high quality food and wines if we can get them cheaply. But cheap food and wine come at a cost hidden behind the branding that companies create to make us feel good about our choices. It is the environmental cost, the price we pay with our ill health and the burden of cheap labor as families struggle to make a living, working on farms and in factories locally and globally, their suffering hidden from our sight.[9] The question is, What we are willing to sacrifice?

Wonder and Awe

When Jesus performed his first miracle, transforming water into an abundance of choice wine, he revealed to his followers that he was the Messiah, God's anointed, who would bring about God's redemption. The prophet Isaiah had spoken of God's future as a feast with rich food and choice wine for all people. The prophet Hosea envisioned God's redemption as a wedding banquet that includes all living creatures. And the prophet Amos imagined the mountains dripping with sweet wine, overflowing with God's abundance. When Jesus performed this first miracle, he stepped in as the bridegroom, wooing his bride and getting her ready for the glorious wedding banquet at the end of time. As you respond to Christ's wooing, walking to the altar to receive him in bread and wine, call upon all your senses to savor the choice wine he offers you and know that you are God's beloved.

Conclusion

N ot all is well with our world. A younger generation is coming of age at a time of profound existential threats, such as climate change and increasing social and political unrest. Anxiety and depression have increased significantly, especially among children and youth. Our Western societies have become increasingly secular, and many of us find ourselves strangers in our homelands. As we watch the steady decline in church attendance, seminaries closing their doors, and a younger generation unable to identify with their parents' belief systems, it is tempting to give in to hopelessness and despair. Where is God in these tumultuous times? Should we just resign ourselves to this trend and enjoy our lives as best as we can? Or should we struggle against the trend and fight like good and brave soldiers?

Growing up in the Lutheran faith, I found Martin Luther's teachings inspirational. His emphasis on God's grace as he searched for a merciful God brought so much freedom to him and those he taught—for centuries to come. He strongly believed that the gospel of Jesus Christ could and should shed its radiant light into the darkness and brokenness of his times. The challenging question for us is to see how our culture is broken and where the gospel can shed its radiant light, and trust that our small loaves and fishes are enough as we offer them up to God for the life of the world. We cannot save the world. Only God can do that. But we can and must return to the center of our faith, rediscover the joy that comes from following Christ, and learn to inhabit his kingdom together as his beloved bride.

Robert Putnam, a political scientist at Harvard University, took a careful and well-researched look at America's social fabric and what has caused its steady and unrelenting decline. His book *Bowling Alone* has become an iconic work in contemporary society, both to uncover its fraying social fabric and to stimulate thoughtful action to rebuild community.[1] As part of his research, he also explored religious participation and found that "faith communities in which people worship together are arguably the single most important repository of social capital in America."[2] This is an incredible statement and worth pondering. The church has had a powerful impact on society.

And yet church attendance has dropped from about 70 percent in 1990 to less than 50 percent in 2020.[3] With this drop a new kind of spirituality has emerged that is highly individualized, rooted in psychology and consumerism, and oriented toward greater personal fulfillment and a quest for the ideal self. One's individual expression of the faith finds fulfillment in privatized forms, anchored in personal preferences.[4]

Can the church once more become the kind of spiritual community that can help transform society and repair its fraying social fabric? American religious historian Martin E. Marty has his doubts: "Unless religious impulses find a home in more than the individual heart or soul, they will have few long-lasting public consequences."[5] It is difficult to build vibrant and close-knit communities that stretch beyond one's immediate family when one's personal preferences take center stage. The spiritual cocktail that Christianity has been mixed into seems to have little room for Jesus' invitation to pick up our crosses and follow him (Matt. 16:24). Self-denial for the sake of others is a difficult concept to disentangle in contemporary culture. The historically oppressed in society were forced into a servitude that was justified by talk about Christian self-denial. And the consumerist vision that life is about self-realization also has little to commend to such puzzling statements as "those who lose their life for [Christ's] sake will find it" (Matt. 16:25). It seems counterintuitive. And yet the full gospel is both good news and a radical and demanding turn toward Jesus Christ and his kingdom, embracing his ways of doing things and slowly but surely shedding ours.

From Scarcity to Abundance

For much of my adult life, I was relatively poor. But I always had a roof over my head and enough to eat. After studying economics, I worked as a missionary and realized that theology is much more interesting than working in a bank, and I felt a strong pull toward missions. With two master's degrees and a PhD in theology, I landed a teaching position and found myself with yet another tight budget, though one with a little more wiggle room. Then a door opened for me to write. For many years I lived on a meager research grant so I could research and write about what I felt called to do. I learned to become resourceful. In all those years, I ate well and enjoyed my wine. My meals were never extravagant, and I did not eat out much. I enjoyed gathering friends and strangers in humble homes, often sharing my home with roommates. Only three years ago, at the age of fifty-two, did I get married and move into a household with a wine fridge and plenty of guest rooms. I still chuckle at that, and my hospitality can now take on more lavish forms.

When we walk to the altar to receive the Lord's Supper, we are taken up into a new community and a new way of consuming: we become part of the body of Christ, and as we consume Christ in bread and wine, we also are being consumed into his church. William Cavanaugh expressed this powerfully: "The Eucharist effects a radical decentering of the individual by incorporating the person into the larger body. In the process, the act of consumption is turned inside out, so that the consumer is consumed."[6] We now belong to God as his people, embracing the ways of his kingdom, where things run differently, counterintuitively.[7]

Some of us are called to leave our fathers and mothers, our brothers and sisters, and follow Christ into different parts of the world, like I did (Luke 14:26). Some of us are called to stay put and learn what it means that our family now includes many more members. Jesus compares the kingdom of God to a great banquet that he invites us to join (vv. 15–24). Are we willing and ready to make his kingdom our home? If so, then he will ask us to throw parties just like he did and invite those who cannot repay us, for our reward lies like a treasure hidden at the end of time (vv. 12–14).

What we consume, how we consume, and with whom we consume reveal much about what we believe the meaning and movement of life to be. Living in a consumer society, we are constantly bombarded by advertisements that lure us into buying things. We have limited resources, and there is so much that we desire. Our culture constantly pulls us to live in the pursuit of things. But what is it that we really need? What is it that Christ is calling us to?

As Christians we inhabit the world of our culture and we inhabit the kingdom of God. Our challenge lies in inhabiting these worlds in such a way that we are part of the Holy Spirit's movement to bring heaven down to earth, not just in our prayers but also in the ways we consume: "Our Father, who art in heaven, hallowed be Thy name. Thy kingdom come, Thy will be done, on earth as it is in heaven. Give us this day our daily bread."

The Lord's Supper and the Lord's Prayer teach us to consume redemptively. God calls us to be free from the enslavement of things, and he invites us to consume in ways that do not oppress and enslave those who grow our foods and make the things we consume. God's forgiveness and healing that we receive in the Lord's Supper is not just for ourselves. It should touch all aspects of our lives, especially our habits of consumption, so that healing can flow to those who are downtrodden by our ways of consumption. When you go to Trader Joe's and a buy lovely Sicilian wine or olive oil that seems rather cheap, you also have to consider that Sicily is known for using undocumented migrant workers from Africa who live in horrific conditions and are being exploited. The burden and cost lie with those enslaved by fate and the vulnerabilities of being refugees. Our seeming abundance is their poverty.

What if we consumed less but learned to invest our resources in those foods and wines that bring healing not only to us and our barren soils but also to those who labor so hard to produce them? What if we helped turn scarcity into abundance, and oppression into dignified living conditions for agrarian workers? Doing so would make our lives more difficult and complicated because we would have to reevaluate our consumer habits. The Greek word for repentance literally means "coming after your thinking and turning your thinking around." In the consumer societies we live in, where oppression is obscured by shrewd marketing, we can pick up our crosses and learn to consume redemptively. It will take sacrifice, and we will never be able to do it perfectly, but we can start small and join a vibrant community of believers that envisions God's redemption reaching into all spheres of society, even in the crafting and enjoyment of a well-crafted glass of wine. When Jesus taught his followers about the ways of his kingdom, he told them a parable about a woman who took yeast and mixed it in with flour until all of it was leavened (Matt. 13:33). Small and hidden consumer choices can have a great impact as God multiplies our offerings and allows them to transform a dark and broken consumer world.

Communion

Everyone's journey is different, and we each get to play different parts as Christ renews his church and plays his part in ten thousand places. We can't be perfectionistic, but we all have a role, however small it might be, in bringing heaven down to earth, sip by sip and bite by bite. As I have pondered over the years what it means to be faithful to Christ during these unsettling and tumultuous times, the words of Eugene Peterson have come back to me again and again: "Gisela, whatever you do, do not neglect to practice hospitality. Don't hesitate to ask for help, and let others bring things to the feast. Share the costs and labor and spread the table often."

A new wine shop opened in our town just as the pandemic started. Brandon and Trent, the owners, are of a younger Christian generation, and they do things differently. They see the wine world as their vocation. The wines they sell are either organic or biodynamic. They work closely with small importers who are intimately connected to the vintners they source their wines from. This web of personal relationships gives them confidence that they source their wines ethically. The challenge with many of the value-driven budget wines in the American market, according to Trent, is that you cannot trace them back to one producer. Most of them are produced conventionally and not sustainably, and we know little about the conditions of the agrarian workers that make such cheap wines possible. These wines are also less healthy because of the large amount of pesticides, fertilizers, and additives used in making the wines. No wonder they cause so many headaches.

Brandon and Trent are part of a younger Christian community that cares about what they consume. They consume less, but what they consume is of higher quality. They support each other in their small artisan endeavors and have rooted themselves in a community that is willing to support them. They are inspired by the Slow Food movement and the natural wine movement, and their mission is to lure a younger generation into enjoying wines, and away from drinking hard liquor, which is so prevalent in the American South. Three years later, their wine shop and wine bar is well attended, mostly by younger people who want high quality wines that are vibrant and expressive and even ethereal. Their wines are not cheap, but Brandon and Trent work hard to find wines of expression that are in the twenty- to thirty-dollar range. Each month, they carefully select an Under $100 Five-Pack that is a more affordable option for their young clientele with limited budgets. That is our price range when we shop for wine. In Europe we would pay half that price because wine is considered a food and not a luxury and is therefore less expensive. In our household we decided to drink less in order to experience a heightened sense of pleasure as we savor our wines more thoughtfully. For God gave wine to make glad our hearts and enjoy the world that he made so beautifully.

When God came down from heaven to become a human being and walk among his people, Jesus spent a lot of his time eating and drinking with saints and sinners alike. Close-knit community life was naturally woven into the fabric of society as people lived in small villages, towns, and cities where they walked everywhere and connected more easily face to face. Just as alcohol is a difficult subject in our time since the introduction of mass-produced hard liquor, so is community more difficult since the introduction of modern technology, whether it is the car that made moving into the suburbs possible, the TV that entertains us at night, or the social media that connect us virtually. Each generation has new challenges, and we must continue to ask how the gospel can shed its radiant light into the dark and broken parts of our society. Most of Jesus' ministry was done outside the traditional religious context, in people's homes, by lakes, and on hillsides. These were small and humble settings, but they were potent for the way the kingdom of God works.

As we carefully curate our wine selection on a limited budget, we open our suburban home as a place of gathering and building community. The wine cup reserved for Elijah turned into Jesus' promise at the Last Supper that he would not drink again from the wine-filled cup until we are reunited with him in his Father's kingdom instills hope in us and a deep longing intermingled with joy. We can bring heaven down to earth in our small gatherings around food and wine, where rich conversations unfold and the healing of our souls can happen. As we bring our humble offerings, we await the fulfillment of things in the world to come. We live in heightened anticipation that God will prepare a great banqueting table where we will savor choice wine from the best vintner of all. Let us worship God with all of our senses as we sip from the eucharist cup and await the future with expectant hope and infectious joy.

Appendix 1

Instructions for Holding a Wine Tasting as a Spiritual Practice

What you need: For each guest, a wineglass, a water glass, a plate for simple bread, and a container (spittoon) in which guests can pour wine that they don't want to finish.

What wines to get: I recommend you get between four and six different wines. If you can, work with a local wine shop that offers a wide range of wines from different regions. I like to use traditional and easily available grape varieties such as Chardonnay, Sauvignon Blanc, and Riesling for the white wines, and Pinot Noir, Chianti Classico from the Sangiovese grape, Cabernet Sauvignon, and Bordeaux blend (Cabernet Sauvignon, Merlot, Cabernet Franc, Petit Verdot, Carménère, and Malbec) or a Côtes du Rhône blend (usually made from Grenache Noir, Syrah, and Mourvèdre) for the reds. Begin with the whites, moving from dry to sweet, and then drink the reds, beginning with the lighter reds and moving toward the more full-bodied ones. You can start with a sparkling wine if you wish. Serve your guests some water and bread between tasting the whites and the reds to cleanse their palettes.

How much time will it take: Because you want to create a contemplative atmosphere where guests can enjoy and savor not only the wine but also thoughtful conversation and a convivial atmosphere, I recommend spending at least one and a half hours to taste four wines, and at least two hours for six.

Create an atmosphere with few distractions, such as music, fragrant candles or flowers. Keep it simple because you want to focus your senses of touch, smell, and taste on the wine. We tend to get easily distracted by visuals and trivial conversations. Allow guests to concentrate on tasting the wine and savoring it.

For each wine you taste, offer a meditation to help your guests embrace the wine tasting as a spiritual practice. Following are the meditations I usually use, and you can add to them or change them as you see fit.

1. Meditation for the First Wine: To Drink Is to Pray
- To drink is to pray, but to binge drink is to sin (a German proverb).
- Simone Veil, a French mystic, once said that attention in its highest form is prayer.
- Let us be prayerful as we approach these wines and learn to pay attention to them with our noses attuned to smell and our tongues attuned to taste.

2. Meditation for the Second Wine: The Priesthood of All Drinkers
- Introduce guests to the concept of the priesthood of all drinkers: we all have been given the capacity to smell and taste, and we need to develop the confidence that we can smell and taste wine on our own terms. Give your guests permission and confidence to do so. Experts can contribute to our understanding but can also be intimidating in how they speak about wine and weaken our confidence.
- God has endowed us with an incredible capacity to taste and smell. The average person has between two and ten thousand taste buds, and each taste bud has between fifty and 150

taste-receptor cells. We have millions of olfactory receptor cells, and these expand from our noses to the back of our throats and integrate the process of tasting and smelling. Ponder this great capacity and invite your guests to pay more attention to these senses of taste and smell.

- The complexity of flavors in our world is a gift of great abundance, and yet so often it goes unnoticed and moves us not. Give your guests room to be moved and touched by what they touch, taste, and smell. Do not be afraid of silence.

3. Meditation for the Third Wine: The Gift of Holy Tipsiness

- Invite your guests to think about allowing their relationship with alcohol to heal and mature.
- Mention the importance of temperance.
- Gentle intoxication gives us the gift of conviviality.
- We learn to relax a little and let go of our need to hold up a façade, pretending we have it all together.
- Reflect on the gift of providing an atmosphere of trust where guests can put down their masks and pretenses and learn to be vulnerable and receptive.
- To be known for who we are and to experience acceptance and love are among the greatest gifts we can give to one another.
- Reflect on the gift of more intimate and caring community.

4. Meditation for the Fourth Wine: The Gift of Place

- Reflect on what it means to be at home in the world.
- Wine helps us to connect to particular places.
- The vintner becomes a mediator between God and place, and facilitates our connection with place. Thoughtful vintners "listen" to the particular places they cultivate, and seek to craft wines that reflect the beauty of these places.
- Why this is important: in a globalized world, we need to reconnect with the local and the particulars of this world.

Crafting and drinking wines that reflect particular places can help us reconnect with the importance of the local and of paying attention to the local.

5. Meditation for the Fifth Wine: Wine and the Great Finale (Eschatology)

- Read Matthew 26:29: "I tell you, I will never again drink of this fruit of the vine until that day when I drink it new with you in my Father's kingdom" (also found in Luke 22:18).
- Whenever we drink a glass of wine, it should remind us that we still await the fulfillment and completion of all things in the future. We are a people of hope. And this should instill in us a holy restlessness that the fulfillment of things is still to come. Learn to savor wine and cultivate hope for God's future.
- Pray: "Come, Lord Jesus, come and deepen our longing for your kingdom."

6. Meditation for the Sixth Wine: Wine Is God's Way of Kissing Humanity

- Think about how intimate an encounter it is with God's creation when we sip a well-crafted wine. It can also be an intimate encounter with our Creator God.

As you bring your own reflections to a close, allow the convivial atmosphere to gather momentum and enjoy watching your guests have good conversations, joyous moments, and meaningful encounters with each other, and hopefully also with God.

Appendix 2

A Biblical and Theological Reflection on the "True Vine" of John 15

I am the true vine, and my Father is the vinegrower. . . .
I am the vine; you are the branches.
—John 15:1, 5

M any people have asked me to offer an interpretation of and reflection on John 15:1–17 and how this passage might fit into the theology and spirituality of wine as I have explored it in my previous works. What does this rich agricultural metaphor, used in the gospel of John, have to do with wine? It might be surprising to you that it has little to do with wine in John's gospel. Yes, it draws on viticulture and uses the vine metaphor. But I would like to argue that it is the context of John's gospel and the Old Testament that imbues this metaphor with potent meaning. Some interpreters see here a reference to the Eucharist. I think this seems unlikely.[1] Then what is it about? And how far can we stretch this metaphor beyond the meaning of its immediate context to speak into our context and the challenges we face?

Earlier in this book, I talked about the New Testament being the vine, the branches, and the fruit while the Hebrew Scriptures are the rootstock. To understand the layers of meaning of this rich and organic metaphor of the vine, one has to understand how it is used in Hebrew Scripture and elsewhere in the New Testament and then carefully look at how John embeds it in his gospel.[2] Only then would I like to offer some reflections on how the message of this passage might speak to us today.

Jesus as the True Vine and the Father as the Vinegrower

When Jesus speaks of himself as the true vine (just as he spoke of himself as the true bread from heaven earlier), he compares himself with Israel as the vine (Ps. 80:8–17; Ezek. 15:2–6; Jer. 2:21; Hos. 10:1) or vineyard (Isaiah 5; 27:2–6; Mark 12:1–9). Jesus is now the true Israel, God incarnate (the tree of life becomes a vine),[3] and those who are grafted into Christ, those who identify with Christ, now belong to and are the true people of God. The Father as the vinegrower in verse 1 evokes the tender love language of Isaiah 5:1–2. The Father now tends lovingly to the vine (his beloved son) and its branches (his beloved church).

Jesus and his followers were intimately familiar with nature and the work of a vinegrower and would have easily understood the many parallels between the world of viticulture and the development and growth of the early Christian community. The threefold image of vinegrower, vine, and branches gives this metaphor its distinctive complexity, reminding one of Paul's image of the body of Christ and its members (Rom. 12:4–5; 1 Cor. 6:15; 12:12–27). This organic metaphor highlights a profound interdependence, intimate union, and fruitful symbiotic relationship between God the Father, Christ, and his followers, the church.[4] It reflects the strong sense of community that early Christianity lived and cherished. It is a reality that is hard for us to grasp since our times are marked by a focus on the individual and how we grow as individuals rather than seeing ourselves as part of a tight-knit community and how we grow closer to Christ by growing closer to each other. Our family of origin might or might not be tight-knit, but this passage certainly invites us to envision ourselves as part of a tight-knit Christian community that is held together by Christ himself.

Judgment and Cleaning

The young Christian community that chose to follow Christ is not spared the work of the vinegrower. The Father removes those branches that bear no fruit (John 15:2).[5] During the winter months, the vinegrower performs one of his most important works: the branches that do not put out new shoots the vinegrower cuts off during dormancy. They are dead wood because of pest infestation, frost, or perhaps a disturbance in growth. These branches have to be cut off to keep the vine healthy and to improve the fruitfulness of the vine. It takes great skill and experience to remove those branches to allow the young branches to grow and bear fruit.[6]

All that the dead wood is useful for is to be burnt in the fire (John 15:6, similar to Ps. 80:16; Ezek. 15:6). Most passages in the Old Testament referring to the vine and vineyard speak about its corruption and God's judgment, so for the early church, it would not have been surprising to hear this word of judgment in relation to the vine.

The second action of the Father is of a vinegrower who prunes/cleanses[7] the branches that bear fruit so that they might bear even more fruit. What does the pruning/cleansing metaphor here mean? Jesus clarifies this in the next verse. It is Jesus who moves to action: he prunes the branches by continuing to cleanse his followers/the church by his word even though they have already become clean: "You have already been cleansed by the word that I have spoken to you" (John 15:3). This resonates with the somewhat cryptic saying earlier in the gospel, when at the foot washing Jesus proclaims, "One who has bathed does not need to wash, except for the feet, but is entirely clean" (13:10). The cleansing here refers to Christ, who purified the disciples by his word.[8] It is Jesus' teaching including who he is and how he brings about God's kingdom that pulsates through the vine, that cleanses and brings life and nourishment to the branches. This reminds me of Hebrews, where the Word of God is described as living and active, sharper than any two-edged sword, judging the thoughts and intentions of the heart to make room for Christ and his grace (Heb. 4:12–16).

The Call to Abide

And what are the disciples to do? What is their role? Here we come to a remarkable section of this extended and organic metaphor of the vinegrower, the vine, and the branches. Nowhere else in the New Testament do we see such a repeated emphasis on the importance of abiding in and dwelling with Christ. Eleven times is the word *abide* used in this passage. It is like a cascading waterfall, pouring forth the loving and urgent invitation and command to persevere in the disciples' abiding in Christ. It is an invitation to a beloved and intimate relationship with Christ and each other in the face of hardship, temptation, persecution, and yes, raw hatred from the world (John 15:18–26).[9] To abide here means to be completely and continually dependent on Christ. As the disciples remain in this intimate union with Christ and each other, they come to know Christ better (v. 15) and can reflect the fruit of Christ: his love, his character, and his way of bringing about God's kingdom through his sacrificial death (vv. 9–14). It is the Holy Spirit, the Spirit of truth, the advocate and comforter who abides with the disciples and teaches them to remain in Christ and his words. And it is the Spirit who teaches them the ways of Christ (John 14:17, 25; 16:6, 13–14).[10] This continued emphasis on abiding urges believers to internalize and make their own the very real and dear presence of Christ in their midst. To cling to Christ in all circumstances is the challenge and command of this passage.

The theological emphasis of this whole passage lies in this urgent call to abide in Christ, his love, and his Word. It is a call to perseverance. It is an urgent call to remain a close-knit community that roots itself in Christ, his self-giving love, and his ways of bringing about the kingdom. This is how the disciples continue to draw life and nourishment from Christ and live like Christ in a hostile environment, offering the fragrant aroma of Christ's eternal life to the surrounding world. And the call to abide in Christ is organically linked to the disciples' ability to bear fruit. The two go hand in hand.

What Kind of Fruit?

What is this fruit that Jesus speaks of? It is fruit that only Christ can produce in the disciples, and apart from him, without abiding and remaining close to him, the disciples can do nothing. (John 15:4). All that the disciples will do has to be marked by a spirit of love and obedience to Christ's word and his commandments: "As the Father has loved me, so I have loved you; abide in my love. If you keep my commandments, you will abide in my love.... This is my commandment, that you love one another as I have loved you. No one has greater love than this, to lay down one's life for one's friends. You are my friends if you do what I command you" (vv. 9–14). Just as Christ loved sacrificially, so are the disciples called to love sacrificially. Just as Christ washed the disciples' feet, so are the disciples called to serve one another in love by abasing themselves. The Christ hymn in Philippians 2 resonates deeply with this call to self-giving love modeled by Christ himself.[11]

And those who keep Christ's command to love one another are the ones who make their permanent home with him, are able to internalize the self-giving love of Christ and live within its orbit. It is a commitment to love as Christ loved, and it is the Spirit who enables them to love sacrificially.[12] It does not come naturally. It is a supernatural gift that flows from Christ's veins into the veins of the disciples.[13] And this beautiful and rich communal life, marked by self-giving love, is not an end in itself. It is for the life of the world (John 6:51).

This kind of fruitful life stands in stark contrast with the sour fruit of the vine and vineyard that the prophets spoke about. In Isaiah, the leadership in Jerusalem and Judah is overcome with greed, hoarding property, and exploiting the poor. They spend their time feasting and getting drunk with wine while the poor suffer (Isa. 3:14–15; 5:8–12).

In John's gospel, Jesus cleanses the temple because it had become infested by a lucrative business industry. Merchants were leeching off the pilgrims who had come to worship at the temple (John 2:13ff). And perhaps it was a challenge to the Jerusalem aristocracy that controlled the temple. They were exploiting the sacrificial system to make a profit and through it distorted the real purpose of sacrifice as a vehicle of prayer.[14] The temple was a branch that needed to be removed and was replaced by Christ himself. Jesus Christ, the vine, is now the great high priest who leads his followers into true worship (John 4:23–26; Heb. 4:14).[15]

To his disciples, Jesus presents a model of love and service that reveals God's character. And perhaps no one understood this better than the apostle Paul, who had deeply internalized what it means to be unified with Christ and abide in him. (See, for example, Rom. 6:5; Gal. 2:20). He also reflected on what a fruitful life in Christ must look like. He called the believers in Ephesus to stop getting drunk on wine and to be filled with the Holy Spirit, cultivating a life of prayer and gratitude instead (Eph. 5:18–20). And in Galatians, Paul emphasizes that the fruit of the Spirit must include all those things that will ensure the flourishing of a decidedly Christian community: love, joy, peace, patience, kindness, generosity, faithfulness, gentleness, and self-control. It is by bearing with one another and forgiving one another that we fulfill the law of Christ (Gal. 5:22–23; 6:2; Col. 3:13–17).

This beautiful and potent extended metaphor of "I am the vine; you are the branches" invites us to live as Christ lived and modeled life for us. It can inspire and strengthen us as we desire to learn how to receive wine as a gift from God. Let's learn to do it with a spirit of faithfulness, generosity, and self-control, for all gifts were given for the flourishing of our communities. God blesses us so that we can be a blessing through this precious gift of wine.

In appendix 3, I offer some reflections on how we can learn to do this well.

Appendix 3

Discussion Guide for Developing a Healthy Drinking Culture

Begin a conversation in your family, church family, or the community you feel comfortable being with about wine as a gift from God and how to develop a wholesome relationship with it. Over time, different cultures have created some helpful guidelines for the consumption of wine. My hope is that we can have a wider conversation in North America about this and develop some guidelines that will protect us and give us a safe space in which we can enjoy wine as God intended.

Consider the following suggestions:

- Every time you enjoy a glass of wine, remind yourself that it is a gift from God.
- Drink with other people, and keep enjoying wine alone to a minimum.
- Savor wine slowly; don't drink it too quickly.
- If you are thirsty, quench your thirst with water first, and then drink wine for enjoyment.

- Limit your drinking to one or two glasses per day for women and two to three for men.
- Drink wine mainly in the context of a meal, and learn how to pair wine with food.
- If you do drink hard liquor, whether straight or in a cocktail, drink it sparingly and only occasionally.
- Consider drinking only after 5:00 p.m., unless it is a special day like Sunday and you are enjoying a festive lunch to celebrate the day of rest that God has given us. Other exceptions would include special feasts, such as Christmas, Easter, and Pentecost, and special occasions, such as weddings, birthdays, and anniversaries.
- Try not to drink wine every day, and build in times of fasting from alcohol, such as certain weekdays or seasons like lent or "dry January."
- When you feel stressed, anxious, or worried, call a friend or someone who might be able to help you. Do not reach for wine or alcohol to ease your stress.
- When you are in a season of working through emotional pain, it is better to abstain from wine and alcohol, because alcohol can easily detach you from the arduous process of getting in touch with unwelcome and difficult emotions.
- Be careful about drinking alcohol at work and with colleagues. Be cautious about letting your guard down.
- Drink coffee or tea or other nonalcoholic beverages at a children's party to model a restrained life of alcohol consumption.
- Be grateful for those moments when you can pause to savor a glass of wine with others.

Please remember that these are just suggestions; I am not trying to lay down a law here. However, I have found these guidelines to be very helpful, and I hope that they can encourage you to set boundaries to help you develop a joyous and life-giving relationship with wine. Remember, to drink is to pray. Wine was always meant to help us commune not just with each other but also with the giver of all good gifts, God himself.

Notes

Chapter 1: Jesus among the Vines

1. Megan Broshi, *Bread, Wine, Walls, and Scrolls*, Journal for the Study of the Pseudepigrapha Supplement Series 36 (New York: Sheffield Academic Press, 2001), 147–48.
2. Flavius Josephus, *The Wars of the Jews*, book 3, chap. 3.
3. See Biblical Archaeology Society Staff, "One of Civilization's Oldest Wine Cellars?" Biblical Archaeology Society, November 22, 2013, www.biblicalarchaeology.org/daily/tel-kabri/one-of-civilizations -oldest-wine-cellars/.
4. Pliny, *Natural History*, vol. 4, trans. H. Rackham, 10 vols. (Cambridge, MA: Harvard Univ. Press, 1968).
5. See my chapter "From Intimidation to Appreciation" in Gisela Kreglinger, *The Soul of Wine* (Downers Grove, IL: InterVarsity Press, 2019).

Chapter 2: Beginnings

1. See Gisela Kreglinger, *The Spirituality of Wine* (Grand Rapids: Eerdmans, 2016), 11ff. The definitive work on this was written by German vintner and theologian Lothar Becker, *Rebe, Rausch und Religion: Eine kulturgeschichtliche Studie zum Wein in der Bibel* (Münster: LIT Verlag, 1999).
2. See www.britishmuseum.org/collection/object/W_1928-1010-3.
3. James Owen, "Earliest Known Winery Found in Armenian Cave," National Geographic, January 12, 2011, www.nationalgeographic .com/culture/article/110111-oldest-wine-press-making-winery -armenia-science-ucla.

4. His drinking foreshadows the feasting that is to come in the Hebrew Scriptures. The Hebrew word for drinking (*shata*) is the stem for the Hebrew noun for feasts and celebrations (*meshteh*).

5. Of course verses like Prov. 31:6–7 must be understood in light of other verses such as Prov. 20:1; 23:20–21; 23:31–35. Proverbs in no way encourages drunkenness but suggests that those who are in bitter distress take a strong drink, probably to get over the shock. To know how to drink wine and deal with alcohol takes much wisdom, and this is why wisdom in Proverbs is personified as a woman who knows how to mix her wine (Prov. 9:2). Those who get drunk are not wise (Prov. 20:1). It is remarkable how much time Proverbs devotes to drinking wine wisely and even describes the state of drunkenness to deter the young from getting drunk (Prov. 23:30–35).

6. This is a difficult passage because the judgment is spoken over Ham's son Canaan instead of Ham himself without any explanation.

7. *Eden* in Hebrew means "pleasure and delight."

Chapter 3: Fulfillments

1. See Lev. 26:3–6. The prophets will reiterate this vision later. See Mic. 4:4.

2. These are rough guesses but are important for gaining some understanding of the proportions. See Carey Walsh, *The Fruit of the Vine: Viticulture in Ancient Israel* (Winona Lake, IN: Eisenbrauns, 2000), 111–12. See also Gustav Dalman, *Arbeit und Sitte in Palästina: Brot, Öl und Wein*, vol. 4 (Hildesheim: Georg Olms Verlagsbuchhandlung, 1964).

3. The nutritional value of wine includes calories, vitamins, and minerals. On wine as a staple, see Nathan MacDonald, *Not Bread Alone: The Uses of Food in the Old Testament* (Oxford: Oxford Univ. Press, 2008), esp. 61.

4. Most of the wines in Egypt had to be imported and were reserved for the upper class. The lower class drank beer, a side product from grain growing. See Tim Unwin, *Wine and the Vine: An Historical Geography of Viticulture and the Wine Trade* (London: Routledge, 1991), 68–71; Robert Curtis, *Ancient Food Technology*, vol. 3 (Leiden: Brill, 2001), 145–46.

5. How destructive this detachment from food production and producers has been is discussed by William Cavanaugh, "Detachment and Attachment," in *Being Consumed: Economics and Christian Desire* (Grand Rapids: Eerdmans, 2008).

6. On the history of the loss of topsoil, see David Montgomery, *Dirt: The Erosion of Civilizations* (Berkeley, CA: University of California Press, 2012). On the Western diet and its negative effect on human health, see Michael Pollan, "The Western Diet and the Diseases of Civilizations," in *In Defense of Food: An Eater's Manifesto* (New York: Penguin, 2008), and Norman Wirzba, "Eating in Exile: Dysfunction in the World of Food," in *Food and Faith: A Theology of Eating* (Cambridge: Cambridge Univ. Press, 2019). On how Western farming practices and global food politics have been destructive in other parts of the world, see Vandana Shiva, *Stolen Harvest: The Hijacking of the Global Food Supply* (Lexington, KY: University Press of Kentucky, 2016).

7. See Gisela Kreglinger, *The Spirituality of Wine* (Grand Rapids: Eerdmans, 2016), 24.

8. See Ex. 23:14–19; 34:18–26; Lev. 23:1–44; Deut. 16:1–17. See also Walsh, *Fruit of the Vine*, 228–47.

9. There are many more festivals that the Israelites were commanded to keep, such as the Feast of Unleavened Bread, the Feast of Firstfruits or the Feast of Weeks, also called the Feast of Harvest, a feast that also commemorated the giving of the Ten Commandments. Traditionally, these feasts would have been joyous celebrations in these agrarian communities. See Exodus 23, Leviticus 23, Paul H. Wright, ed., *Rose Guide to the Feasts, Festivals and Fasts of the Bible* (Carol Stream, IL: Rose Publishing, 2022) and *Feasts of the Bible* (Carol Stream, IL: Rose Publishing, 2004) for a brief overview.

Chapter 4: Mission Failed, God's Judgment, and Renewed Promise

1. See also Lev. 23:22; Ex. 22:22; Deut. 10:17–19; 24:17–19; 27:19 for more examples.

2. See Gisela Kreglinger, *The Spirituality of Wine* (Grand Rapids: Eerdmans, 2016), 27.

3. Kreglinger, *Spirituality of Wine*, 28ff.
4. See Lev. 26:3–6.
5. Thank you to Mary DeJong for this phrase.
6. See Gerard Manely Hopkins' poem "God's Grandeur."
7. See Richard Bauckham, *The Bible and Ecology: Rediscovering the Community of Creation* (Waco, TX: Baylor Univ. Press, 2010); Fred Bahnson and Norman Wirzba, *Making Peace with the Land: God's Call to Reconcile with Creation* (Downers Grove, IL: InterVarsity Press, 2012); Douglas J. Moo and Jonathan A. Moo, *Creation Care: A Biblical Theology of the Natural World* (Grand Rapids: Zondervan Academic, 2018); and Rabbi Yonatan Neril and Rabbi Leo Dee, *Eco Bible*, vol. 1, *An Ecological Commentary on Genesis and Exodus* (Interfaith Center for Sustainable Development, 2020). Even Pope Francis devoted an entire encyclical letter to it: *Laudato Si': On Care for Our Common Home* (Rome: Libreria Editrice Vaticana, 2015).
8. For a helpful introduction to this from a historical perspective, see Richard Bauckham, *Living with Other Creatures: Green Exegesis and Theology* (Milton Keynes, UK: Paternoster, 2012).
9. See also Joel 2:23–24.
10. See also Joel 3:18.

Chapter 5: The Bridegroom Is Here

1. Gisela Kreglinger, *The Spirituality of Wine* (Grand Rapids: Eerdmans, 2016), 218ff.
2. Fyodor Dostoevsky, *The Brothers Karamazov* (New York: Knopf, 1992), 360.
3. Dostoevsky, *Brothers Karamazov*, 361–62.

Chapter 6: When the Saints Sipped Wine

1. Gisela Kreglinger, *The Spirituality of Wine* (Grand Rapids: Eerdmans, 2016), 42.
2. For a helpful introduction to this, see John D. Zizioulas, "The Early Christian Community," in Bernard McGinn, John Meyendorff, and Jean Leclercq, eds., *Christian Spirituality: Origins to the Twelfth Century* (New York: Crossroads, 1997), 23–43.

3. For a careful discussion of this, see Gordon Fee, *The First Epistle to the Corinthians* (Grand Rapids: Eerdmans, 1987), 531–58.

4. Kreglinger, *Spirituality of Wine*, 32.

5. Irving Woodworth Raymond, *The Teaching of the Early Church on the Use of Wine and Strong Drink* (New York: AMS Press, 1970), 92–95.

6. *The Letters of St. Cyprian III*, ed. G. W. Clarke (ACW 46; New York: Newman Press, 1986), 98.

7. *Letters of St. Cyprian III*, 104.

8. *Letters of St. Cyprian III*, 98–103.

9. For a detailed discussion, see Raymond, *Teaching of the Early Church*. For an overview, see Kreglinger, *Spirituality of Wine*, 38–43.

10. Kreglinger, *Spirituality of Wine*, 42.

11. Kreglinger, *Spirituality of Wine*, 43.

12. Desmond Seward, *Monks and Wine* (New York: Crown, 1979), 21.

Chapter 7: When the Saints Planted Vineyards

1. Saint Benedict, *The Holy Rule of St. Benedict*, trans. Leonard J. Doyle, OSB, chap. 53, https://archive.osb.org/rb/text/rbeaad1.html#53. Accessed March 9, 2024.

2. Ibid., chap. 31, https://archive.osb.org/rb/text/rbemjo1.html#31. Accessed March 9, 2024.

3. Timothy Frey, ed., *The Rule of St. Benedict in Latin and English with Notes* (Collegeville, MN: Liturgical Press, 1981), chap. 40.

4. Saint Benedict instructed the monks to stop seven times a day for prayer as part of the monastic office, now also called the liturgy of the hours or the divine office: "'Seven times in the day,' says the Prophet, 'I have rendered praise to You' (Ps. 119:164). . . . Let us therefore bring our tribute of praise to our Creator." *Holy Rule of St. Benedict*, chap. 16, https://archive.osb.org/rb/text/rbefjo2.html#16. Accessed March 9, 2024.

Chapter 8: Tipsy Monks and the Fragrance of the Reformation

1. Bernard of Clairvaux, quoted in Marianne Schlosser, ed., *Geheimnisvolle Gegenwart: Eucharistische Gebete* (Sankt Ottilien: EOS Verlag, 2015), 103. Translation from the German mine.

2. Alois Thomas, *Die Darstellung Christi in der Kelter* (Düsseldorf, Germany: Schwann, 1981), 24.

3. Desmond Seward, *Monks and Wine* (New York: Crown, 1979), 26–28.

4. See chap. 14 on this contentious issue.

5. Benedict of Nursia, *St. Benedict's Rule for Monasteries*, trans. Leonard J. Doyle (Collegeville, MN: Liturgical Press, 1948), chap. 53, quoting Matt. 25:35, www.gutenberg.org/files/50040/50040-h/50040-h.htm#chapter-53. Accessed June 6, 2023.

6. Ibid., chap. 36, quoting Matt. 25:36, www.gutenberg.org/files/50040/50040-h/50040-h.htm#chapter-36. Accessed June 6, 2023.

7. For a more detailed discuss of wine and its role in medical care during Christendom, see Gisela Kreglinger, *The Spirituality of Wine* (Grand Rapids: Eerdmans, 2016), 164–79.

8. "Bernard of Clairvaux's Apologia," in World History Commons, https://worldhistorycommons.org/bernard-clairvauxs-apologia. Accessed June 5, 2023.

9. Kreglinger, *Spirituality of Wine*, 49–50.

10. *Cru* is a French term that is usually translated as "growth" and designates a particular parcel of land in relation to its qualities for growing vines. Burgundian vintners use it to this day (*Premier Cru* and *Grand Cru*). Other wine regions such as Germany have adopted this term into their system as *Großes Gewächs*.

11. Hugh Johnson, *The Story of Wine* (London: Mitchell Beazley, 1989), 130.

12. For a detailed discussion of the theological meaning of this meal expressed in its symbolism, see Kreglinger, *Spirituality of Wine*, 88–95.

13. See "Letter E Depicting the Grain Harvest," Getty Images, www.gettyimages.com/detail/news-photo/initial-capital-letter-e-depicting-the-grape-harvest-news-photo/142085233?adppopup=true.

14. Schlosser, ed., *Geheimnisvolle Gegenwart*, 103. Translation from the German mine.

15. This particular sermon has not been translated into English yet. For an introduction to Johannes Tauler, see Johannes Tauler, *Sermons* (New York: Paulist Press, 1985).

Chapter 9: Martin Luther and John Calvin Sipped Wine

1. John Calvin, *Institutes of the Christian Religion*, 2 vols., trans. James Anderson (Edinburgh: Calvin Translation Society, 1847), 3.10.2, 1:720–21.

2. Martin Luther, *The Judgment of Martin Luther on Monastic Vows*, LW 44:252. See Gisela Kreglinger, *The Spirituality of Wine* (Grand Rapids: Eerdmans, 2016), 52.

3. For more information about the women of the Reformation and their roles, see Roland Bainton, *Women of the Reformation* (Minneapolis: Fortress, 1971).

4. Martin Luther to Katherine Luther, July 29, 1534, in *The Letters of Martin Luther*, trans. and ed. Margaret A. Currie (London: Macmillan, 1908), 299.

5. See Jim West, *Drinking with Calvin and Luther! A History of Alcohol in the Church* (Lincoln, NE: Oakdown, 2003, 29ff.

6. Martin Luther, WA 10/III. Translation mine.

7. West, *Drinking with Calvin and Luther*, 35. See also 33–34.

8. Jancis Robinson, *The Oxford Companion to Wine* (Oxford: Oxford Univ. Press, 2006), 150–51.

9. West, *Drinking with Calvin and Luther*, 54–55.

10. John Calvin, *Institutes of the Christian Religion*, 2 vols., ed. John T. McNeill, trans. Ford Lewis Battles (Philadelphia: Westminster, 1960), 3.19.9, 1:841.

11. Calvin, *Institutes*, 3.10.2, 1:720–21.

12. John Calvin, *Commentary on the Book of Psalms*, 5 vols., trans. James Anderson (Edinburgh: Calvin Translation Society, 1847), 4:155–57.

Chapter 10: The Mayflower and the Promised Land without Wine

1. Ulrich Zwingli, *Zwingli and Bullinger*, vol. 24 of Library of Christian Classics, ed. G. W. Bromiley (London: SCM, 1953), 75, 111, 185–238.

2. For a list of references to Knox's writings about wine, see Gisela Kreglinger, *The Spirituality of Wine* (Grand Rapids: Eerdmans, 2016), 239n87.

3. Gregory A. Austin, *Alcohol in Western Society from Antiquity to 1800: A Chronological History* (Santa Barbara, CA: ABC-Clio Information Services, 1985), 134, 163, 171, 174.

4. Ibid., 180. See Puritan Philip Stubbes's book *The Anatomy of Abuses*, in which he speaks out against visiting prostitutes, lending money at interest, gluttony, and drunkenness.

5. John Bunyan, *The Pilgrim's Progress* (Peabody, MA: Hendrickson, 2004), 45.

6. Ibid., 48, 127, 128, 199, 222.

7. Thomas Pinney, *A History of Wine in America: From the Beginnings to Prohibition* (Berkeley: University of California Press, 1989), 9–11.

8. Ibid., 29.

9. For a more detailed account, see ibid., 13ff.

10. George Washington, *The Complete Works of George Washington* (n.p.: Madison and Adams Press, 2017), 706.

11. Ibid., 847.

12. To curb heavy drinking and increase revenue in England and Scotland, parliament started to increase the duty on strong spirits beginning in 1760. This resulted in less destructive drinking habits. This date also marks the beginning of the Industrial Revolution. However, many distilleries went underground to avoid taxation, and the Scots continued to drink heavily. See Austin, *Alcohol in Western Society*, vol. 2, 335–63.

13. "Ten Facts about the Distillery," George Washington's Mount Vernon, www.mountvernon.org/the-estate-gardens/distillery/ten-facts-about-the-distillery/.

14. The French heavily taxed wine, and liberation came to be associated with fewer taxes and more affordability of wine for the common people. See Noelle Plack, "Intoxication and the French Revolution," Age of Revolutions, December 5, 2016, https://ageofrevolutions.com/2016/12/05/intoxication-and-the-french-revolution/.

15. Thomas Jefferson to Monsieur de Neuville, December 13, 1818, in *The Writings of Thomas Jefferson*, vol. 15, ed. Andrew A. Lipscomb and Albert Ellery Bergh (Washington, DC: Thomas Jefferson Memorial Association, 1904), 178. See Kreglinger, *Spirituality of Wine*, 187–88.

16. See John Hailman, *Thomas Jefferson on Wine* (Jackson: University Press of Mississippi, 2006).
17. Thomas Jefferson to William Johnson, May 10, 1817, in *Thomas Jefferson's Garden Book*, ed. Edwin Morris Betts (Philadelphia: American Philosophical Society, 1944), 572.
18. See Kreglinger, *Spirituality of Wine*, 60–61, and W. J. Rorabaugh, *The Alcoholic Republic: An American Tradition* (Oxford: Oxford Univ. Press, 1979), 104–6.
19. Rorabaugh, *Alcoholic Republic*, 53–56.
20. Robert C. Fuller, *Religion and Wine: A Cultural History of Wine Drinking in the United States* (Knoxville: Univ. of Tennessee, 1996), 75. See also Rorabaugh, *Alcoholic Republic*, 87. The number declined after 1830 because of the increase of large distilleries and a reduction in production, and rapid industrialization set in.
21. Rorabaugh, *Alcoholic Republic*, 69.
22. Ibid., 76–68. Chapter 3, "The Spirits of Independence," traces whiskey production and sales and whiskey as an exchange commodity.
23. Ibid., 126–35.
24. Ibid., 90–92.

Chapter 11: The Jewish Passover Meal

1. See Luke 2:41–52. See also Exodus 12–13.
2. Lev. 23:9–14.
3. Mic. 4:4.
4. Exodus 12; Leviticus 23.
5. Ps. 115:14–16.
6. In Ezekiel 47 the prophet sees water flowing from the temple. See also Joel 3:18. Historical descriptions of the temple in the second century BC show that water featured prominently in the Second Temple. See David Stubbs, *Table and Temple: The Christian Eucharist and Its Jewish Roots* (Grand Rapids: Eerdmans, 2020), 70–71.
7. Ps. 116:1–2.
8. By the time of Jesus, it had become custom to drink four cups of wine during the Passover celebration. For a summary of the development of the Passover throughout its history, see Baruch M. Bosker,

"Unleavened Bread and Passover, Feast of," in David Noel Freedman, *Anchor Bible Dictionary* (New York: Doubleday, 1992), vol. 6, 755–65. See also Abraham P. Bloch, *The Biblical and Historical Background of the Jewish Holy Days* (New York: Ktav Publishing House, 1978).

9. Ps. 104:15.

10. Ex. 12:27.

11. Gen. 9:4; Lev. 17:11; Deut. 12:23.

Chapter 12: Sacrifice, Blood, and the Wine Cup Just for Elijah

1. In Psalm 50, God asks his people, "Do I eat the flesh of bulls or drink the blood of goats? Offer to God a sacrifice of thanksgiving, and pay your vows to the Most High " (vv. 13–14). God does not need a sacrifice from his people, for the whole world belongs to him and all the animals in it (vv. 10–12). It is humans who need the reality of sacrifice, because it reveals to them their need for redemption and instills awareness of their creatureliness and their profound dependence on God and all that he gives to them. While substitutionary ideas are an important part of Israel's sacrificial system, there are other important aspects to consider that relate not to humans but to the nonhuman world, especially animals. See Ex. 13:13–15; Lev. 1:3; Num. 8:18; 3:12–13.

2. Robert Farrar Capon, *The Supper of the Lamb: A Culinary Reflection* (New York: Smithmark, 1996), 48.

3. See Richard Bauckham, *Living with Other Creatures: Green Exegesis and Theology* (Milton Keynes: Paternoster, 2012), 99–101.

4. Margaret Visser, *The Rituals of Dinner* (New York: Grove Weidenfeld, 1991), 32. If you don't believe it, just google CAFO (concentrated animal feeding operations) and ponder whether God would approve of these.

5. In Christian theology, one cannot separate the body from the soul; they are one single unit, designed to work in harmony.

6. Gisela Kreglinger, *The Spirituality of Wine* (Grand Rapids: Eerdmans, 2016), 73ff.

7. Ben Sira, *The Wisdom of Ben Sira: A New Translation with Notes by*

Partrick W. Skehan, trans. Patrick W. Skehan (New York: Doubleday, 1987), 385.

8. To this day, medical scientists study and write about the health benefits of wine when consumed in moderation. See Kreglinger, *Spirituality of Wine.*

9. Each family was to offer one fourth of a hin of wine as a drink offering, approximately one bottle of wine. See Lev. 23:13; Num. 15:5.

10. See Pss. 116:17–18 and 104:14–15 for the inspiration for this traditional prayer.

11. Luke 2:43, 46.

12. Ex. 12:42.

Chapter 13: Wine and the Lord's Supper

1. Matt. 21:8–11; John 12:13.

2. For a helpful introduction to how the body holds our wounds and scars, see Bessel van der Kolk, *The Body Keeps the Score: Brain, Mind, and Body in the Healing of Trauma* (New York: Penguin, 2014).

Chapter 14: Christ, the Noble Grape

1. The neurosciences have done considerable research into how the brain processes smells, emotions, and memories and how these are connected. See Gisela Kreglinger, *The Spirituality of Wine* (Grand Rapids: Eerdmans, 2016), 108–10.

2. See also Gen. 1:11–12; 9:3; Ps. 104:14; 107:37–38; 147:8; Ezek. 34:26–27; Zech. 8:12; Matt. 6:30; 1 Cor. 3:7; 2 Cor. 9:10.

3. For a more careful discussion of how vintners experience the wine-crafting process as a spiritual journey, see Kreglinger, *Spirituality of Wine*, 121–42.

4. On the different stances toward the Lord's Supper during the Reformation, see Kreglinger, *Spirituality of Wine*, 68–69, and especially footnote 7. For an accessible introduction to the different positions, see Gary Macy, *The Banquet's Wisdom: A Short History of the Theologies of the Lord's Supper* (Akron, OH: OSL Publications, 2005), 170–227.

5. See Robert Taft, *Beyond East and West: Problems in Liturgical Understanding* (Washington, DC: Pastoral Press, 1984), esp. 61–80.

Chapter 15: Sensing Salvation

1. Jean Anthelme Brillat-Savarin, *The Physiology of Taste: Or Meditations on Transcendental Gastronomy*, trans. M. F. K. Fisher (1949; New York: Vintage Classics, 2011), 48.

2. Our senses of smell and taste also serve to protect us from eating spoiled and poisonous food.

3. Alexander Schmemann, *For the Life of the World* (New York: St. Vladimir's Seminary Press, 1973), 11. See also Gen. 1:29–31.

4. Gisela Kreglinger, *The Spirituality of Wine* (Grand Rapids: Eerdmans, 2016), 101ff.

5. Robert W. Jenson, "How the World Lost Its Story," *First Things*, October 1993, 37.

6. Thomas Aquinas, *Summa Theologica* 1a2ae.27.1ad3, quoted in Neil Campbell, "Aquinas' Reasons for the Aesthetic Irrelevance of Tastes and Smells," *British Journal of Aesthetics* 36, no. 2 (1996): 168. For a more detailed discussion of this issue, see Kreglinger, *Spirituality of Wine*, 104ff.

7. See Kreglinger, *Spirituality of Wine*, 108.

8. This has most recently been argued by Edward Slingerland in *Drunk: How We Sipped, Danced, and Stumbled Our Way to Civilization* (New York: Little, Brown Spark, 2021).

9. See Kreglinger, *Spirituality of Wine*, 110.

10. For more on the different perspectives on Christ's presence in the Lord's Supper, see ibid., 67–68, esp. footnote 7.

Chapter 16: Wine Use and Abuse in the Bible

1. Alcohol researchers confirm the positive effects of drinking together in moderation. See, for example, Madeline E. Goodwin and Michael A. Sayette, "A Social Contextual Review of the Effects of Alcohol on Emotions," *Pharmacology, Biochemistry and Behavior* 221 (Nov. 2022): doi: 10.1016/j.pbb.2022.173486. For the adverse effects of drinking alone, see Kasey G. Creswell, "Drinking Together and Drinking Alone: A Social-Contextual Framework for Examining Risk for Alcohol Use Disorder," *Current Directions in Psychological Science* 30 (Feb. 2021): 19–25, doi: 10.1177/0963721420969406.

2. For a helpful study of these dynamics, see Carey Ellen Walsh, "Under the Influence: Trust and Risk in Biblical Family Drinking," *Journal for the Study of the Old Testament* 25, no. 90 (2000): 13–29, doi.org /10.1177/030908920002509002.

3. Noah curses Ham's son Canaan harshly for it, and this story has puzzled interpreters for millennia. What exactly was Ham's transgression? Why was his son Canaan judged so severely for his father's transgression? Interpreters continue to puzzle over these questions. What is clear, though, is that the text does not judge Noah for getting drunk but only the son who responds by not protecting and preserving his father's dignity, instead spreading the news and therefore shaming his father in public.

4. Bathsheba receives a place of honor in the genealogy of Jesus in Matthew's gospel, where only four women are named and singled out among forty-two generations mentioned. See Matthew 1.

5. Deuteronomy sets forth harsh punishment for youth given to drunkenness (Deut. 21:18–21).

Chapter 17: Moonshine Hangover

1. Irving Woodworth Raymond, *The Teaching of the Early Church on the Use of Wine and Strong Drink* (New York: AMS Press, 1970), 110.

2. For short and interesting articles on the fascinating history moonshine in the South, see Clair McLafferty, "A Brief History of Moonshine," Mental Floss, December 4, 2015, www.mentalfloss .com/article/71993/brief-history-moonshine; Oxford Treatment Center, "History of Moonshine and Prohibition in the United States South," Oxford Treatment Center, updated July 14, 2023, https://oxfordtreatment.com/substance-abuse/alcohol/history-of -prohibition-and-moonshine/.

3. Robert Fuller, *Religion and Wine: A Cultural History of Wine Drinking in the United States* (Knoxville: Univ. of Tennessee Press, 1996), 75.

4. See Gisela Kreglinger, *The Spirituality of Wine* (Grand Rapids: Eerdmans, 2016), 58–64.

5. W. J. Rorabaugh, *The Alcoholic Republic: An American Tradition* (Oxford: Oxford Univ. Press, 1979), 7–8.

6. Fuller, *Religion and Wine*, 75.

7. See Kreglinger, *Spirituality of Wine*, 58–64.

8. Rorabaugh, *Alcoholic Republic*, 21.

9. "Temperance Movement Cartoon: The Drunkard's Progress, 1826," Gilder Lehrman Institute of American History, www.gilderlehrman .org/history-resources/spotlight-primary-source/temperance -movement-cartoon-drunkards-progress-1826.

Chapter 18: Some Sobering Thoughts on Alcohol Use and Abuse

1. Kate Julian, "America Has a Drinking Problem," *The Atlantic*, July/ August 2021, www.theatlantic.com/magazine/archive/2021/07 /america-drinking-alone-problem/619017/.

2. To read up on these interviews, see Gisela Kreglinger, *The Spirituality of Wine* (Grand Rapids: Eerdmans, 2016), 121–63, 199–213.

3. How does one find reliable information about alcohol consumption in the USA? Surveys are not reliable because consumers often do not provide reliable data. The University of Adelaide has collected an amazing amount of data, gathered by many academic researchers in the field, and provides us a good understanding of drinking habits around the world. See the Wine Economics Research Centre databases (https://economics.adelaide.edu.au/wine-economics/databases); and Kym Anderson, Signe Nelgen, and Vicente Pinilla, *Global Wine Markets, 1860 to 2016: A Statistical Compendium* (Adelaide, AU: Univ. of Adelaide Press, 2017), www.adelaide.edu.au/press/titles/global-wine -markets. Wine consumption continues to increase in the USA. See "US Wine Consumption," Wine Institute, https://wineinstitute.org /our-industry/statistics/us-wine-consumption. These statistics include the production, export, and import of alcohol.

4. For a comparative study, see Hannah Ritchie and Max Roser, "Alcohol Consumption," Our World in Data, April 2018, last revised January 2024, https://ourworldindata.org/alcohol-consumption. See also Todd Love, Christian Laier, Matthias Brand, Linda Hatch, and Raju Hajela, "Neuroscience of Internet Pornography Addiction: A Review and Update," *Behavioral Sciences* 5, no. 3 (2015): 388–433, www.mdpi.com/2076-328X/5/3/388/htm. In my book *The*

Spirituality of Wine I discuss the rise of addiction and argue that it is a systemic problem of our society rather than only the plight of individuals. I offer some introductory reflections on the reasons that might lie behind it. See "Wine and the Abuse of Alcohol," in Kreglinger, *Spirituality of Wine*, 180–98.

5. "Alcohol-Related Deaths Increasing in the United States," National Institutes of Health, January 10, 2020, www.nih.gov/news-events /news-releases/alcohol-related-deaths-increasing-united-states.

6. In 2018, 36.9 percent of college students engaged in binge drinking. See "Alcohol Facts and Statistics," National Institute on Alcohol Abuse and Alcoholism, last updated February 2020, www.niaaa.nih .gov/sites/default/files/AlcoholFactsAndStats.pdf#. See also "College Drinking," National Institute on Alcohol Abuse and Alcoholism, October 2020, www.niaaa.nih.gov/sites/default/files/publications /NIAAA_CollegeDrinking_Oct2020.pdf.

7. "Key Substance Abuse and Mental Health Indicators in the United States: Results from the 2021 National Survey on Drug Use and Health," Substance Abuse and Mental Health Services Administration, December 2022, www.samhsa.gov/data/sites/default/files/reports/rpt 39443/2021NSDUHFFRRev010323.pdf.

8. "Alcohol Abuse Statistics," National Center for Drug Abuse Statistics, https://drugabusestatistics.org/alcohol-abuse-statistics/.

9. "Drinking Trends in the UK," Alcohol Change, https://alcohol change.org.uk/alcohol-facts/fact-sheets/drinking-trends-in-the-uk.

10. See "Alcohol Consumption," Our World in Data, April 2018, last revised January 2024, https://ourworldindata.org/alcohol -consumption#global-consumption-of-spirits. Scroll down to the category of "Alcohol Consumption by Type of Alcoholic Beverage."

11. "Alcohol Abuse Statistics," National Center for Drug Abuse Statistics, https://drugabusestatistics.org/alcohol-abuse-statistics/.

12. See "Alcohol Abuse Statistics," National Center for Drug Abuse Statistics, https://drugabusestatistics.org/alcohol-abuse-statistics/ under the subheading "Analysis: Trends in Alcohol Abuse." Males are more prone toward it than females, and this behavior usually peaks at twenty-one years of age.

13. See, for example, "Alcohol Abuse Statistics," National Center for Drug Abuse Statistics, https://drugabusestatistics.org/alcohol-abuse-statistics/.

14. *Avalon* came out in 1990 and was directed by Barry Levinson. Since its release, circumstances have only worsened. It is a truly prophetic film with a sobering message, calling Americans back to the table and the social connectedness that it brings.

15. Kasey G. Creswell, Yvonne M. Terry-McElrath, Megan E. Patrick, "Solitary Alcohol Use in Adolescence Predicts Alcohol Problems in Adulthood: A Seventeen-Year Longitudinal Study in a Large National Sample of US High School Students," *Drug and Alcohol Dependence* 2022: doi:10.1016/j.drugalcdep.2022.109552.

Chapter 19: Some Sobering Stories on Alcohol Use and Abuse

1. Gabrielle Glaser, *Her Best-Kept Secret: Why Women Drink—And How They Can Regain Control* (New York: Simon and Schuster, 2013), 9.

2. Holly Whitaker, *Quit Like a Woman: The Radical Choice to Not Drink in a Culture Obsessed with Alcohol* (New York: Dial Press, 2019), 67. Whitaker is quite critical of Alcoholics Anonymous and espouses a recovery program more suitable for women. For another popular author retelling her journey from alcoholism to a sober life, see Annie Grace, *This Naked Mind*. Though it is an imbalanced assessment of the scientific studies available, it's helpful in understanding a new generation of women who are struggling with alcohol abuse.

3. Canadian psychologist Bruce Alexander argues that the structures of our free-market Western societies foster addictive behavior and disorders. Bruce Alexander, *The Globalization of Addiction: A Study in Poverty of Spirit* (Oxford: Oxford Univ. Press, 2008). For a brief introduction to his book, see the chapter "Wine and the Abuse of Alcohol" in Gisela Kreglinger, *The Spirituality of Wine* (Grand Rapids: Eerdmans, 2016), 191–92.

4. John Calvin, *Commentary on the Book of Psalms*, 5 vols., trans. James Anderson (Edinburgh: Calvin Translation Society, 1847), 4:155–57. Martin Luther, WA 10/III.

Chapter 20: Lady Wisdom Plants a Vineyard

1. Thomas Jefferson in a letter to de Neuville, December 13, 1818, in *The Writings of Thomas Jefferson*, vol. 15, ed. Andrew A. Lipcomb and Albert Ellery Bergh (Washington, DC: Thomas Jefferson Memorial Association, 1904), 178.

2. For a discussion of the vintner as a practicing theologian, see chapter 6 of Gisela Kreglinger, *The Spirituality of Wine* (Grand Rapids: Eerdmans, 2016), 121–63.

3. Brenda Foster and Jeffrey Colman Salloway, eds., *The Socio-Cultural Matrix of Alcohol and Drug Use: A Coursebook of Patterns and Factors* (Lewiston, NY: Edwin Mellen Press, 1990), 2–3; and David J. Janson, *Preventing Alcohol Abuse: Alcohol, Culture, and Control* (London: Praeger, 1995), 32–36, 39, 50–51.

4. William T. Cavanaugh explores this brilliantly in his little but profound book *Being Consumed: Economics and Christian Desire* (Grand Rapids: Eerdmans, 2008).

5. Theologically it matters who produces what we consume and how it is produced. Exploitative practices, often purposefully hidden behind the marketing façades of corporate companies, go against the gospel and the call to love and care for our neighbors. Those who produce what we consume are our neighbors in the biblical sense. See Lev. 19:11–16 and Cavanaugh, "Detachment and Attachment," in *Being Consumed*, 33–58.

6. "Number of Bonded Wineries in the United States in 2022, by State," Statistica, www.statista.com/statistics/259365/number-of -wineries-in-the-us-by-state/.

7. One even wrote a memoir about it: Adam McHugh, *Blood from Stone: A Memoir of How Wine Brought Me Back from the Dead* (Downers Grove, IL: InterVarsity Press, 2022).

Chapter 21: Wine to Gladden the Human Heart

1. William Wordsworth bemoans this in his poem "The World Is Too Much with Us."

2. Alexander Schmemann explores this beautifully in his book *For the Life of the World* (Crestwood, NY: St. Vladimir's Seminary Press,

1973), 11–46. On the priestly function of vintners, see, "The Vintner as (Practicing) Theologian: Finder or Maker?" in Gisela Kreglinger, *The Spirituality of Wine* (Grand Rapids: Eerdmans, 2016), 121–42.

Chapter 22: On Earth as It Is in Heaven

1. See the chapter "Wine and Communal Feasting: The Joy of the Lord Is Our Strength" in Gisela Kreglinger, *The Spirituality of Wine* (Grand Rapids: Eerdmans, 2016), 83–99, esp. 88–95.

Chapter 23: Savoring Ourselves into Wonder

1. See my discussion in Gisela Kreglinger, *The Spirituality of Wine* (Grand Rapids: Eerdmans, 2016), 80–82. This might in part be because there have been so many disputes around the Lord's Supper and how to interpret it. See my discussion in *Spirituality of Wine*, 68–67, including footnote 7.
2. See John Cassian's discussion on gluttony in John Cassian, *The Institutes* (New York: Newman Press, 2000), 117ff. Cassian interpreted Paul's teaching on the "flesh" as the physical body rather than the sinful urges of our lives.
3. See Kreglinger, *Spirituality of Wine*, 103.
4. See the Slow Food website: www.slowfood.com. Carlo Petrini, Slow Food's founder, has written several books that explain their mission and devotion to the pleasure of eating and drinking.
5. I recommend you look for a local wine shop that will help you find those treasures. You can also find them online. Most of us have a limited budget, and a good wine shop with helpful staff can find those treasures for an affordable price.
6. See the Jones Valley Teaching Farm website for inspiration: https://jvtf.org/.
7. See Double Up Food Bucks' website: www.doubleupal.org/.
8. See Christopher Carter, *The Spirit of Soul Food: Race, Faith and Food Justice* (Urbana, IL: Univ. of Illinois Press, 2021).
9. For a discussion of the injustice woven into our global food system, see "The Global and the Local," chapter 3 in William T. Cavanaugh, *Being Consumed: Economics and Christian Desire* (Grand Rapids: Eerdmans, 2008), 59–88.

Conclusion

1. Robert D. Putnam, *Bowling Alone: The Collapse and Revival of American Community*, revised and updated (2000; New York: Simon and Schuster, 2020).
2. Ibid., 66.
3. See Jeffrey M. Jones, "U.S. Church Membership Falls below Majority for First Time," March 29, 2021, Gallup, https://news.gallup.com/poll/341963/church-membership-falls-below-majority-first-time.aspx.
4. Putnam, *Bowling Alone*, 73–74.
5. Professor Martin E. Marty of the University of Chicago, quoted in Putnam, *Bowling Alone*, 69.
6. Cavanaugh, *Being Consumed*, 95.
7. In the gospel of Mark, the theme of "the way" is really important and teaches us that Jesus' ways are very different from our ways and hopes and expectations. Reorienting ourselves toward God's kingdom and the ways of the kingdom is an important part of Christian discipleship and crucial for maturing in the Christian faith.

Appendix 2

1. See Craig Keener and Richard Bauckham for a detailed argument on this point, both of whom agree that here we do not find a reference to the Eucharist. Craig Keener, *The Gospel of John: A Commentary*, vol. 2 (Grand Rapids: Baker Academic, 2003), 990, 996. See also Richard Bauckham, *The Testimony of the Beloved Disciple: Narrative, History, and Theology in the Gospel of John* (Grand Rapids: Baker Academic, 2007), 256ff. Bauckham argues in relation to John 6:51 that though Jesus' cryptic allusion here is indebted to eucharistic language, the focus of this passage is on the movement from Christ's incarnation (Jesus as the bread that came down from heaven) to the cross (Jesus as the bread that gives for the life of the world). The Incarnate One, who took on flesh, is the one who needs to shed his blood. Bauckham argues that "the transition in v. 51c is not from faith to the Eucharist as the means of eternal life, but from believing in Jesus to believing in Jesus as the one who died a violent death for the life of the world." Richard Bauckham, *Gospel of Glory: Major Themes in Johannine Theology* (Grand Rapids: Baker Academic,

2015), 97–100. See also Meredith J. C. Warren, *My Flesh Is Meat Indeed: A Non-Sacramental Reading of John 6* (Minneapolis: Fortress, 2015). For the disciples and the early church, it was a hard truth to accept that the Messiah, the incarnate Christ, would have to suffer a violent death to save the world. See also Mark's gospel where the disciples struggle to accept that Jesus has to die.

2. For a helpful introduction to reading John in light of the Old Testament, see Claus Westermann, *The Gospel of John in the Light of the Old Testament* (Peabody, MA: Hendrickson, 1998).

3. See also Col. 1:15–20.

4. Lothar Becker, *Rebe, Rausch und Religion: Eine kulturgeschichtliche Studie zum Wein in der Bibel* (Muenster, Germany: LIT Verlag, 1999), 194.

5. The same Greek word is used earlier in John for Jesus' cleansing the temple (2:16). It is also used in Eph. 4:31 and 1 Cor. 5:2, among other places.

6. German theologian and vinegrower Lothar Becker has inspired these reflections. See Becker, *Rebe, Rausch und Religion*, 192.

7. The Greek word used here means both pruning and cleansing, and it is not a common expression from viticulture. Keener, *Gospel of John*, 996.

8. Bauckham, *Testimony of the Beloved Disciple*, 256.

9. Keener argues that this whole section (John 15:1–17) functions as a unit contrasted with the world's hatred. Keener, *Gospel of John*, 988. Thank you to Randy Frazee. Our conversation inspired these reflections.

10. See also Keener, *Gospel of John*, 999. In Mark's gospel, the disciples continually resist the idea that their Lord will have to suffer and die, and yet here John brings it home to them once more through the organic metaphor of the vine that emphasizes the life (fruit) that will come from his sacrificial death.

11. Earlier in the gospel, Jesus refers to bearing fruit in light of his own death. He then calls his disciples to follow him by "hating their lives": serving as Christ served (John 12:24–25).

12. In the Bread from Heaven Discourse, Jesus also emphasizes his sacrificial love: he will die for the life of the world (John 6:51).

13. The apostle Paul reflects in a similar way: "It is no longer I who live, but it is Christ who lives in me. . . . I live by faith in the Son of God, who loved me and gave himself for me" (Gal. 2:20 NRSV 1995).

14. Richard Bauckham, *Living with Other Creatures: Green Exegesis and Theology* (Milton Keynes, UK: Paternoster, 2012), 99.

15. Keener, *Gospel of John*, 520–25. As I've already mentioned, the same Greek word that describes the Father's removing branches from the vine is used earlier in John for Jesus' cleaning the temple (2:16). And Jesus speaks of his own body as the new temple (John 2:21).

Companion Bible Study for Your Church or Small Group

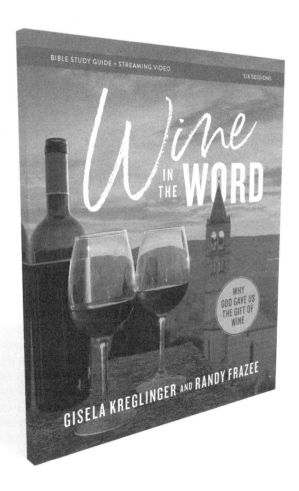

AVAILABLE NOW
and streaming online at StudyGateway.com

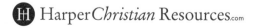